HALINA
FAITH IN THE FIRE

by Elwood McQuaid

"When thou passest through the waters, I will be with thee; and through the rivers, they shall not overflow thee; when thou walkest through the fire, thou shalt not be burned, neither shall the flame kindle upon thee. . . . Fear not; for I am with thee."
—Isaiah 43:2, 5

HALINA
FAITH IN THE FIRE

by Elwood McQuaid

The Friends of Israel Gospel Ministry, Inc.
Bellmawr, NJ

All Scripture quotations, unless otherwise indicated, are taken from the King James Version.

We would like to express our deepest thanks to our dear friend and colleague Halina Ostik who, many years ago, responded to Elwood McQuaid's request to record her experiences on audiotape with the intent that Elwood would one day turn her remarkable story into a book, to the glory of God. We thank her also for graciously supplying some of the photographs used. We also want to thank our colleague Anna Cieślar who took the cover photograph for us and whose devotion to and knowledge of The Friends of Israel's work in Poland was invaluable in putting together this book.

HALINA: FAITH IN THE FIRE

by Elwood McQuaid

Copyright © 2013 by The Friends of Israel Gospel Ministry, Inc.
Published by The Friends of Israel Gospel Ministry, Inc.
P.O. Box 908, Bellmawr, NJ 08099

Second Printing...2015

Library of Congress Control Number: 2013944941
ISBN-10: 0-915540-52-5
ISBN-13: 978-0-915540-52-5

Cover design by Brenda Kern
Waveline Direct, LLC, Mechanicsburg, PA

Visit our website, *www.foi.org*

DEDICATION

This book is dedicated to David M. Levy, my friend, congenial colleague, and outstanding expositor of Scripture. He is among us as a tower of integrity warmly admired by his peers. Exemplary in David's ministry has been his development of the superb staff and multiple ministries of The Friends of Israel in Poland. This gratitude and admiration are not mine alone, but I speak for all who know him well.

ACKNOWLEDGMENT

Writing is a solitary enterprise. But that fact holds true only in phase one. The finished product is a collaboration of the many minds and skills of intensely qualified people who research, correct, polish, and improve the work until its presentation to a hopefully appreciative readership. Such has been true with *Halina: Faith in the Fire*. My thanks to all who said yes to participate in the process. A special expression of gratitude is due my indefatigable editor, Lorna Simcox, who spent literally hundreds of hours and not a few sleepless nights editing, advising, and shaping the text into what now rests between the covers of this book. To Lorna and all those who believed the story must be told, I give my sincerest thanks. The final stamp of approval and measure of satisfaction derived from invested labor will have to come from the readers. If they say, "Well done," then it's all been worth it; we have our reward.

TABLE OF CONTENTS

FOREWORD

I once asked an Israeli woman who lived in a settlement frequently infiltrated and attacked by terrorists why she chose to stay, because she was often in danger of losing her life. "You must understand our belief," she said, "that out of death comes life. So no matter how many times they try to kill us, we'll plant new life. And in the end, life will win."

Her commitment to believing in the triumph of her cause regardless of personal cost might well explain the essence of this book. It tells the story of an amazing individual who walked through the fires of Hitler's genocidal rampage and survived.

But making it through to live out her remaining years cloistered with collapsed dreams and bitter recollections is not what Halina Ostik's story is about. It is, rather, a confirmation of the fact that no matter how grim and costly the past may be, life on the other side of a vale of tears can become a study in courage, inspiration, and commitment. Above all, it can embody the enduring message of faith, which is the sustaining force that defines a life worth living.

Woven through the fabric of this book is the companion chronicle of a nation marked for death yet doggedly refusing to perish. It is an exposé of every danger free nations are plagued by when radicals move in with a determination to destroy a way of life blessed by peace, prosperity, and a foundation of faith.

The biblical declaration "Blessed is the nation whose God is the LORD" (Ps. 33:12) is readily dismissed today. But it is not an irrelevant, antiquated option. There is evil in the world; and godless forces, if left unchallenged, will rain unimaginable suffering and devastation on innocent people.

The evidence is here. From it, we can learn that forgetting is never smart. In the end, those of us who choose to resist evil, whatever the cost, not only will preserve freedom but pass the treasure of liberty to our heirs. To do otherwise is to turn our backs on the future and forfeit the sacred trust endowed by our Creator.

In this book, those who resisted evil had names that are obscure to most of us here in the West. Yet their courage and tenacity come to us as a legacy of hope we can ill afford to dismiss. In many respects, their story is potentially our own—one filled with dreams and aspirations, trials and obstacles—and, in the end, one worthy of pursuing with every breath we take.

Elwood McQuaid

CHAPTER 1

Faces From the Darkness

She stood for a long time before the steps leading up to the granite and bronze Monument to the Ghetto Heroes sculpted by Nathan Rapoport. Looking back at her were figures of men and women who had fought valiantly against the Nazis. Nearby, people strolled through the lovely park. Winding, paved walkways and graceful trees offered shade and comfort to passersby. It was a pleasant place to get away from the bustle of the city of Warsaw.

"How many," she wondered, "realize where they are walking?" Here in the neighborhood of Muranów, Poland, had stood the Warsaw Ghetto where the Germans caged in 400,000 Jewish people in little more than a square mile. Before the Ghetto uprising in April 1943, they had deported more than 300,000 to be murdered at Treblinka. Although the Jewish people bravely held the Germans at bay for a few weeks, the Nazis prevailed; and the Ghetto was burned to the ground during the infamous days of World War II.

The streets where people were strolling along casually, enjoying a coffee or Coca-Cola, had been piled high with rubble from leveled buildings. Hundreds of Jewish people, unable to escape, were entombed beneath the bricks—the very ones later used to construct the structures surrounding the park. Nearby was a solemn reminder of those terrible days—an apartment building bearing large photographs of some of the victims. A journalist referred to them as the "ghosts of Muranów."

For many people, the monument was primarily philosophical. Not for Halina Peszke Ostik. Gazing up at it was almost like going back in time. She remembered the monstrous orange flames billowing over the Ghetto that had become a giant Nazi inferno, incinerating human beings like sticks of wood. Though Halina was not Jewish, she loved the Jewish people and shared a portion of history with them that could not be erased.

The bronze figure that held her attention the longest was that of a distraught young mother holding a baby. One of her arms was raised, as if to protect the infant somehow. By the time Halina visited the monument, the people it enshrined were long gone. The child represented the only possible survivors—a symbol that all would not be lost and that life would again rise from the ashes. Adolf Hitler had not succeeded in implementing his "final solution to the Jewish question." Nor did he succeed in subjugating Poland forever. But during the Holocaust, no one knew how things would end, certainly not Halina.

⁕

In the summer of 1939, the coming maelstrom could hardly have entered her mind as she and a friend from the British Embassy vacationed at a resort in Huculszczyzna, a seductively beautiful retreat in the Carpathian Mountains. For an attractive 20-year-old craving adventure and exposure to all things beautiful, this place was as near perfect as it could get.

Lush, green valleys carpeted a breathtaking countryside dotted with rustic, rural villages. Flowers filled the fields as far as the eye could see. Waterfalls cascaded over rocky descents, and softly flowing rivers and streams invited visitors to linger and gather memories that would brighten their days long after returning to the mundane world of ordinary life.

Back in Warsaw, things were different. Signs of trouble were everywhere. Squads of workers were digging trenches in strategic locations, hoping to protect the city from the massive Nazi onslaught they knew was coming. Germany, under Hitler's command, had declared war on Poland. As far as the Poles were concerned, it looked like another round of the same style of war they were used to: long lines of mud-filled trenches, soldiers with fixed bayonets plodding past barbed-wire obstacles, and potholes made by artillery used to gain a few feet of ground. But it wasn't.

On September 1, 1939, the people of Warsaw and other major Polish cities were awakened by the whine of German aircraft. Wave after wave of Nazi planes invaded Polish airspace, unleashing an earthshaking thunder of exploding bombs that obliterated everything in their path. The Polish people were being introduced to the German *blitzkrieg* (lightning war).

The *blitzkrieg* defied the norm of conventional warfare. The tactic was to launch massive, full-force attacks designed to crush the opposition quickly and then sweep beyond the defensive positions to destroy everything that might become an obstacle to occupation.

Halina's family was no stranger to war. Her ancestors were people of action and courage. When French leader Napoleon Bonaparte pitted his armies against the Russians, he was aided by the Polish Vistula Legion, an elite force considered the best of the foreign mercenaries fighting with the French. To the Poles, Napoleon represented the hope of reestablishing a free Poland—a cherished objective in the aftermath of being bounced about by conquering rivals who shifted and shrank the country into a buffeted no-man's land. Though the dream was not realized, the hope refused to die.

Halina's grandparents and great-grandparents had

served in the Polish army. They were soldiers, but not fighters. Their commitment was to serve the needs of the troops. Among them was Dr. Samuel Peszke, a surgeon who traveled with Bonaparte's forces. Unfortunately, he was captured by the Russians and spent two years in one of the czar's prisons. Because of his great skill as a surgeon, he was offered a position in the czar's palace. He refused it. Having seen all he wanted of Russia and Russians, he requested and received permission to leave. On the journey away from St. Petersburg, he became enthralled with the beauty of Poland's lush countryside and decided it would be where he and his family would put down roots.

The Poland of Halina's childhood was indeed beautiful. Stunning landscapes, scenic rivers, and quaint villages adorned the countryside. Poland had a certain magnetism that attracted people struggling with illness, fatigue, overwork, and stress, beckoning them to the mountains and seaside resorts to find relief. All that was about to change.

Germany's objective was total war with total success in the shortest possible time. Poland, along with its 3.3 million Jewish people, seemed to be a special case. The Nazis viewed the Poles as racially inferior and therefore unfit to participate in Germany's thousand-year Third Reich. Consequently, they planned to subject the Polish people to a brand of brutality unlike anything that took place during wars between great armies.

⌇

Much to her mother's relief, Halina had returned home from the mountains. But time was running out. German troops would soon overtake the city and plunge Warsaw into chaos. It was September 6, and the colors of fall were still displaying their beauty in sharp contrast to what was going on. Although the bitter winds of the Polish winter had not yet swept in, a storm was on the horizon. Halina was in bed when she felt herself being shaken awake by her mother. The look on Mother's face was enough to tell her something was very wrong. "Get up quickly and get your things together. We must leave as soon as we can."

"But Mother, what's the matter? Why must we leave? And where are we going?" Halina asked.

"It's all over the radio. The Germans are moving into the city, and Polish authorities are telling everyone who can travel to run toward the East. It's especially urgent for the young men to leave before the Nazis can catch up to them."

"What about Zygmund?" Halina asked. Zygmund was Halina's brother. He was older than she, and Halina adored him. Some of her fondest childhood memories revolved around Zygmund. Before her father died in 1925, when she was six, the family led an almost idyllic life. Their flat in those days was in the Praga district near the Vistula River. It was comfortably if not elegantly furnished, and her father's library was large enough to accommodate 4,000 books, which he attended to studiously. It was Father who had instilled in her a love for reading and learning. A well-respected journalist, he taught history in Jewish schools and also managed a student home for boys, many of whom were orphaned during World War I.

The Peszke home had a Bible on every nightstand; and her parents revered its words, which told of God's love for Israel and the Jewish people. So Halina and Zygmund were taught to love the Jewish people, even though anti-Semitism was rampant in Poland. In 1918, after Germany's defeat in World War I, Poland gained its independence. Afterward, anti-Semites launched a reign of terror on the Jews, massacring as many as they could get their hands on.

Later, when the economy faltered, they blamed the Jews; and a new round of anti-Semitic pogroms and boycotts began. But in her home, not a single negative word was ever spoken about the Jewish people.

In fact, it was just the opposite. Although Gentiles, the family lived in the Jewish section of Warsaw and understood the situation of Poland's Jews in the post-World War I period, when most lived in extreme poverty. Many times a day Halusia, as her mother called her, would hear Jewish street merchants calling, "Handele, handele" (bargain, bargain). Too poor to own horses, as the Polish peddlers did, they pulled their heavy carts by straps slung over their shoulders. Her "Mum" explained that they sold bottles, old clothes, and rags for a few pennies to buy a herring and piece of bread for their daily meal.

One day, as mother and daughter walked home from shopping, a door swung open onto the street, and about one hundred Jewish boys ran out. Halina knew immediately they were Jewish because they were dressed in long black coats, black trousers, and black shoes. Each wore a small skullcap (*yarmulke*) on his head and had side curls (*payis*) that tumbled down his cheeks. But it wasn't the clothing that caught her attention. She had seen Orthodox dress many times. It was the color of the boys' skin.

As they ran past, Halina noticed their faces were nearly yellow, not at all plump and rosy like the children at her school. So she asked her mother, "Mum, why are those boys so pale?"

Her mother, a godly, kind Christian who had nurtured her children carefully, quietly replied, "Because their parents are too poor to take them to the country or the seaside, where you and your brother go. They are malnourished and do not get enough of the right kinds of food to keep them strong and healthy." Halina never forgot those pallid faces and promised herself that someday she would take care of Jewish children and make sure they were well fed.

Mother also read to her Halusia. Among the child's favorites was a book titled *Ministering Children* about a family whose mother took her youngsters on outings to poor neighborhoods, bringing food and presents to the boys and girls. Her mother did the same thing. She would take Zygmund and Halusia to the homes of poor families, bringing food and other necessities. Christmas was a favorite time for distributions, when they also went to the Polish children's hospital with gifts they crafted themselves.

Life was much different for the family when Father was alive. There was money enough for excursions and trips to the mountains where she and Zygmund played and made a lifetime of happy memories. For little Halina and her family, the mountains were more than a refuge for recreation and relaxation. Her father had suffered from a heart condition that left him in a state of increasing physical decline. Often, on doctor's orders, they would pack their belongings and go to the mountains for his health.

One of Halina's favorite places was the little village of Rytro by the Poprad River in the south of Poland. There her father spent quiet days reading and resting, while the children played in the fields by the swiftly flowing river. Zygmund even saved someone from drowning there. Halusia told everyone about it. Zygmund was her hero.

⁓

"What about Zygmund? He's in Gdansk working at the library," Halina told her mother. "If he comes home and we are gone, how will he know where to look for us?"

"All I know," her mother replied, "is that the government is assembling a combat force and telling young men where to go. So we'll know at least where he might be and look for him there later. No more questions. We must leave Warsaw immediately. Hurry! Take only what you can carry. There is no transportation, so we will have to walk."

To see her mother in a state of near panic was a new experience for Halina. Ordinarily, she was calm, almost reserved—not the type to be easily frustrated. Today she was different, and the only practical response was to obey.

The escape route was jammed with people from every imaginable walk of life. It was a patchwork of prominent, middle class, poor, and transients, all with one thing in mind: not to fall into the hands of the Nazis. Tugging at Halina's heart was the disparity of ages and conditions within the throng of humanity around her. Some of the elderly were being helped along or carried on makeshift carts. Others were less fortunate and had to do the best they could with whatever strength they could muster.

Most touching were the children. One family had a number of them trailing behind. Several were very young and struggling to keep up. Halina wondered how many of these frightened people could endure the difficult odyssey long enough to reach safety. These thoughts preoccupied her as she looked at her mother. The place they intended reaching on foot was 87 kilometers (54 miles) away. The last thing she wanted was for something to happen to her Mum.

Her mother's life had become difficult enough after Halina's father died. His death had left her shaken and unprepared. She had never worked outside the home, and the only work experience she had before she was married was writing articles for a children's newspaper called *The*

Friend of Children. In the Polish culture of the day, it was rare for a mother to have a job. Father was the breadwinner. Mum looked after the household and nurtured the family.

Losing her husband devastated her. So much so that she suffered a type of breakdown that caused her to be confined to her home. For more than a month, while struggling to recover, she was unable to care for Zygmund and Halina.

Fortunately, Dora Pankerst from the Anglican Church where the family worshiped volunteered to take Halusia with her to the seaside for two weeks. Miss Pankerst served with the Church Mission to the Jews (CMJ). They went to the town of Hel, located on the Polish Baltic Sea.

The place was a child's paradise. Located at the tip of a small peninsula jutting out into the Baltic, it had a beachfront that was a long, wide stretch of sand running down to the chilly waters. Surrounding the town were old bunkers and the remains of gun emplacements from World War I that beckoned children to explore. One could sit there for hours enjoying the antics of the seals frolicking in the sea and watching fishermen casting into the abundant schools of fish that swam near the shore.

As they prepared for the trip, Miss Pankerst told Halusia, "We will not be alone on our journey to the sea. I've asked a young man to come along with us on the trip. I'm sure you will like him, and he'll be someone to keep you company."

"Do you think he will play with me?" asked her small companion.

Dora smiled. "Yes, I'm sure he will be happy to play with you. His name is Victor, and he is very pleasant."

When Victor arrived, he turned out to be just as Miss Pankerst had described. He was much older than Halina.

And he was Jewish, which meant most people at the resort would be unwilling to associate with him.

From the moment they met, the teenaged Victor became like a big brother to the seven-year-old who loved adventure and very much needed a friend. Their days by the Baltic were filled with exciting expeditions through the woods. They explored the crumbling bunkers, played with the lifeless old artillery guns, and looked into the windows of the quaint shops lining the streets.

But their favorite place during those two weeks together was the beach where they spent long afternoons in the sand and water. Victor was always careful that Halina didn't stray too far into the sea, which gave Miss Pankerst peace of mind. The young man was Victor Buksbazen, who later would become the first executive director of The Friends of Israel Gospel Ministry. And the bond God forged between the two of them during those pleasant days by the sea during her mother's illness would last a lifetime.

✍

Halina was devoted to her mother and wanted to make sure she would be safe. They had been on the road only a few hours when they heard the whine of an airplane coming toward them. As it approached, Halina could see the large swastika painted on the side. The pilot flew so close to the ground they could see his face. Suddenly, machine-gun fire from the aircraft began strafing the road, scattering men, women, and children in all directions. Fortunately, most of the roads leaving Warsaw were hemmed in on both sides by thick woods that became a refuge for people scrambling for a safe place to hide. Many more would have died had it not been for the woods.

The refugees from Poland's capital were learning quickly

that the Nazis had no intentions of being benevolent. They unleashed their first exhibition of genocide with unimaginable fury, killing in unprecedented numbers. The invasion of Poland marked the beginning of a time when it made no difference if you were rich or poor, educated or illiterate, Jew or Gentile. To the Nazis, every person on the road was a target; and the Germans would not relent until every Pole was incarcerated, turned into slave labor, or slaughtered.

For Halina and her mother, the destination was the town of Siedlce, near the Nowlny estate of a cousin of Halina's mother. Halina's family circle was large and closely knit. Birthdays and other special occasions drew as many as 80 or more family members who never squabbled or disagreed, even though half the family was Catholic and the other half Protestant. Religion was never an issue, nor was anything else. They were family, and that was what mattered. Halina's mother knew her cousin would be happy to take them in.

It was late in the evening when they reached the city of Minsk Mazowiecki. Already large groups of people were milling around looking for food and somewhere to bed down for the night. As her mother slumped down for a rest, she looked at Halina and asked, "What will we do now?" She was nearly in a state of exhaustion, and Halina knew they must find shelter and warmth from the chilly night air.

"You sit here, and I'll go look for a place for us to sleep," she told her mother. She went from house to house knocking on doors but was constantly turned away. Finally, a door opened, and Halina found herself facing a kind woman asking what she wanted.

"My mother and I have been on the road from Warsaw all day, and I am looking for a place for us to rest, at least for a while."

"Certainly," the woman replied. "Run along and get your mother, and I will get something to warm you up. After that you can stay here with me for the night."

The words were music to her ears, and the thought of a night's rest in a warm bed was wonderful. The next morning, Halina felt refreshed. But it was obvious the previous day's ordeal had left her mum in no condition to walk another 40 kilometers (almost 25 miles) to Siedlce. Unfortunately, no other options were available. Though there were some vehicles on the road, most were filled with people who were in no mood to take on additional riders. So they began the long trek toward their destination.

In the afternoon, Halina spotted a car with only two men inside. They were Polish soldiers—one was a captain. With a prayer on her lips, she approached the vehicle and asked if it were possible for them to ride with the men to her mother's cousin's place in Nowiny.

When the captain answered, "Sure, get in," Halina was certain her ride was a direct answer to her prayer because both she and her mother were at the point where it seemed impossible to take another step on that dreadful road. She was even more convinced when the men asked her where they wanted to go and promised to find the estate for them and drop them off there.

It was hours later when the captain knocked on the door and told Halina's relative he had two visitors for her. As their cousin welcomed them with open arms, the men returned to the vehicle and were gone. The experience reminded Halina of the Bible verse that says some people have "entertained angels unawares." It seemed to her that God had sent His angels to help her. The solders' kindness during her distress was nothing short of amazing. And even if they were not angels, they were close enough to satisfy Halina.

The days with their relatives at the estate were a reprieve from the terror that was beginning to fill their lives. They had places to sleep, ate meals of noodles and beans, and snacked on apples from the orchard. Unfortunately, it was a brief reprieve. On September 11, five days after Halina and her mother arrived, German troops entered Siedlce and began rounding up what they could of the town's 15,000 Jews and killing them. Three years later the remaining 10,000 would be deported to the extermination camp of Treblinka, built by the Germans in occupied Poland. Within the next 13 months, Treblinka would be used without mercy to liquidate 800,000 to 1 million Jewish people.

It wasn't long before Halina heard that German troops were spotted on the nearby road and were herding captured Polish soldiers to who knew where. Because there were obviously no German rations for the Poles, servants were sent to the road with bags of apples to toss to the Polish men as they passed by. Overhead, Stuka dive bombers swooped down so close that everyone was forced to run to makeshift shelters to escape being killed by the explosions.

Halina was worried about the family's children, who were terrified by the bombs and the sight of so many people passing on the roads, carrying all of their worldly belongings and begging for food. She responded by using her Girl Guide skills to teach the youngsters to help her build a bomb shelter. She also invented games to occupy them and keep their minds off what was going on around them.

Halina had joined the Polish Girl Guides (*Harcerstwo*) when she was 12. It was much like the Boy Scouts of America. Founded in 1910 under the leadership of Olga Drahonowska-Malkowska, the program was designed to help girls develop their character and talents, think critically, and work well with others so that they would become mature, patriotic, responsible adults.

They happily sang songs that instilled a love of God and country, an appreciation of nature, and a desire to do good every day. And though the activities seemed more like games, they were serious training. The Girl Guides had to learn every street and alley in Warsaw, information that would prove invaluable during the war. They also attended a month-long Girl Guides' summer camp. Forty girls were divided into teams of six patrols. Each patrol was given an old army tent and had to learn how to pitch it as part of their survival-skills training for life in the wild.

The girls chopped down trees and placed planks on sawed-off tree stumps for beds. They made bed supports from slender pine trees. There were no mattresses, so they learned to improvise by stuffing straw into big bags. After all was in place and they were ready for their first full night out, the girls raised a large mound, installed a pole, and raised the Polish flag. Then they formed a circle around it, sang, and paused for evening prayer.

In the morning, they ate kasha they cooked themselves on a makeshift stove they had built with bricks and topped with a sheet of metal. Bubbling pots of potatoes, vegetables, noodles, and anything close at hand made up the next meal. Neatly scooped out trenches served as primitive but adequate outhouses.

The survival skills the Girl Guides learned masqueraded as games: navigating through the forest without being detected, fleeing quickly through the forest in case of war, being prepared to aid someone else, helping farmers in nearby villages harvest crops.

Halina returned to Warsaw a different girl. She loved

being a Guide. She also learned she could do many new things and do them well. The camp had given her confidence and turned the girls into one big, happy family that would always be friends.

When the Germans arrived, they outlawed Guiding and Scouting; but that did not stop the Guides and Scouts. Working inside the Polish Resistance, the Guides became a key factor in fighting the Nazis. Their first-aid skills were used in medical stations, first-aid posts, and auxiliary hospitals. They were trained to listen for enemy bombers and identify the types of aircraft the Germans were using. They cared for orphans and staffed refugee shelters and centers for lost children. Guides carried supplies to the front lines, planted explosives, and carried out acts of sabotage.

After the Warsaw Ghetto was established, Guides smuggled in food and rescued Jewish children, taking them to homes provided by the Resistance. The skills the girls had learned at camp helped them navigate through enemy-held territory while carrying messages for the Polish underground. Many of the girls would sacrifice their lives. Were it not for the Girl Guides, it is doubtful the Resistance would have been as successful as it was in obstructing the German forces and hastening the end of Nazi aggression in Poland.

ⴵ

Guiding had given Halina the skills to keep her cousin's children busy. As for the adults, nothing could banish the sense that their country was being ground to pieces before their eyes. They were horrified when word came the Germans had surrounded a nearby village, rounded up all of the peasants, and forced them into a single cottage. After locking them inside, they set fire to the building and burned everyone to death.

If Hitler's generals were attempting to instill fear, they were succeeding. Ironically, the peasants they had reduced to ashes were the very people who had held out hope that Germany would perhaps improve their situation. That illusion now was dead. It was clear this would be a fight to the finish; if Germany won, Poland would die.

After a few weeks among friends and relatives, Halina's mother decided it was time to return to Warsaw. The country was occupied by the enemy, and it was now imperative to find a route to survival. Their best chance was to return to the familiar surroundings of the Warsaw apartment, for it seemed only a matter of time before the estate in Nowiny would be overrun with Nazis.

With tears and solemn promises of prayer, Halina and her mother prepared to depart. Their cousin gave them a horse-drawn cart filled with large sacks of flour, carrots, and potatoes. She also sent a man along to guide the horse and protect them on the road. Her provision came as a godsend. For many weeks there was soup and food for the table. They had no money. But prices were so high that people who had a little quickly had none anyway. So, hoping that Zygmund would soon return, they settled into an extremely uncertain life.

CHAPTER 2

One Minute to Live

The Warsaw Halina returned to was not the same warm and carefree place of her childhood. Zygmund had come home, and the happy reunion called for celebration. Otherwise, there was not much to be happy about. The city had become a bleak and dangerous place.

German troops were now in control. There was no electricity, which meant living in the dark. And there was no power to operate the trams, so the search for the necessities of life, which were hard to come by, had to be conducted on foot.

It seemed as though the occupying force had everything under lock and key. One of the first things the Germans did was impose a strict curfew. Anyone on the streets after 8 in the evening was shot. If someone missed curfew by even one minute, he was killed. It was common for people to knock frantically on the doors of strangers, pleading to be let inside because they had misjudged the time and were terrified.

The first winter of the war was the worst. Halina had enrolled in English classes several kilometers from home. With no trams or buses, she made the long, frigid walk wrapped only in a coat better suited for milder weather. On some evenings she feared she would freeze to death. But the lessons gave her a command of the English language that later became a valuable asset.

On the way home, she kept an eye out for scraps of wood she could burn in the stove. That often meant rummaging through the debris of bombed-out buildings. Many nights Halina would open her rucksack and triumphantly empty her bounty on the apartment floor. "Look at what I've brought. It won't be enough to keep a fire through the night, but it is enough to heat soup and warm water for a wash." She and her mother passed their evenings huddled around their small stove, sipping cups of warm soup, grateful for one more day of survival.

Hitler's intentions for the Polish people had been made as clear in his book, *Mein Kampf,* as his intentions for the Jews. To achieve a new, pure, Germanic race, he considered it essential to murder every Jew and Pole who belonged to the intelligentsia. Only the uneducated peasants would be allowed to live and serve as slave labor.

As quickly and by any means possible, the Germans slaughtered the country's political and religious leaders, along with all of Poland's intellectuals. Thousands of teachers, priests, and others in the upper classes were executed en masse. The Nazis wanted to do more than subjugate Polish culture; they wanted to obliterate it.

They also wasted no time in destroying the breathtaking vistas that had captivated Dr. Peszke so long ago. Soon countless numbers of concentration camps and killing factories blighted the landscape, infesting the country like vermin.

As if the German attacks were not enough, the Russians launched an assault to capture eastern Poland. So there were Germans invading on the west, and Russians on the east. Both occupying powers had the same objective: to wipe Poland off the map. Between 1939 and 1945, approximately 6 million of Poland's 35 million people would be killed, 3 million of them Jewish—nearly 90 percent of the country's Jewish population. In addition, more than 90 percent of the Poles killed would be noncombatants targeted by Russians and Germans who deliberately and randomly killed anyone who crossed their paths.

Hitler's plan for refashioning the countryside for the Third Reich was dubbed "Germanization." That meant Polish farmers and landholders were slaughtered or driven off their property and replaced by people exhibiting suitable Aryan qualities. Soon Germanization became evident in public areas: Signs were posted, "Entrance is forbidden to Poles, Jews, and dogs."

In the beginning, the people of Warsaw believed the way to stay alive was to be passive: do no harm and keep a low profile. That fantasy soon evaporated. It became evident their enemy looked for any excuse to kill.

One night two German guards who had been drinking heavily got into a fight with each other, and one of them ended up dead. For the area commander, the situation was a pretext to murder Polish people living nearby. Soldiers were dispatched to enter nearby houses and rouse 100 men from their sleep. The Nazis marched the pajama-clad men into the street, lined them up, and shot them. Soon afterward more people were dragged from their homes and murdered for no specified reason.

The wave of brutality sweeping away Warsaw's people washed over Halina one day when she decided to visit a former professor who lived in an apartment building that catered to university professors. As she approached the building, she could see that all of the doors were open. Seeking an explanation, she called out to a man on the street. "Why are all the doors into the apartment open?"

"It's because there's no one there," the man replied. "They've all been taken away."

"But where have they been taken?"

"The soldiers came and took them," he told her. "The word I have is that they have all been shot."

Halina was horrified. The man she intended to visit was a kind, gentle person who never would have been involved in subversive activities. But that didn't matter to the Germans. Hitler's death squads were complying with the ideology of the masters of the new order.

The Einsatzgruppen

Following the initial invasion by German regular forces in 1939, special-action squads—the *Einsatzgruppen*—were left behind with specific orders to arrest and kill anyone resisting the occupiers. The Einsatzgruppen was a combination of police and Hitler's evil paramilitary, the *Schutzstaffel,* better known as the SS. Tens of thousands of landowners, ministers, and members of the intelligentsia—including government workers, teachers, doctors, dentists, officers, journalists, members of the nobility, and others considered influential—were systematically executed. Halina's friend was among the thousands caught in the Nazi net.

The Einsatzgruppen was created as a special task force to operate in areas previously taken by the army. Its mission was specific. Hitler personally issued orders stating the necessity of eliminating all Poles identified with public Polish positions. "There must be no Polish leaders," he declared. "Where Polish leaders exist, they must be killed."

Hitler's paramilitary hit men were not uneducated. They belonged to the SS, staffed with many scholarly Germans from the intellectual elite of the Nazi party. Of the 25 dispatched to Poland, 15 of them reportedly possessed doctorates, including doctors of jurisprudence and philosophy. Their task was to direct some 3,000 troops operating as "mobile killing units" empowered to murder anyone thought to have tendencies opposing Nazi superiority. There was no due process. No one was given the right to stand before a judge for a hearing. That, in the eyes of SS leader Reinhardt Heydrich, would take too much time. "The people must be shot or hanged immediately without trial," Heydrich said. "The little people we want to spare; but the nobles, priests, and Jews must be killed."

On September 3, two days after the invasion, Heinrich Himmler, the head of the Gestapo and SS, ordered the Einsatzgruppen to shoot all insurgents, defined as anyone who supposedly endangered German life or property. Soon 200 executions a day were reported. By the end of September 1939, an estimated 65,000 civilians had been murdered.

These roving execution squads murdered on a whim and did not confine their victims to those on Hitler's list. In one instance—forever frozen in time by a photograph—a woman stood with her back toward an Einsatzgruppen soldier several feet away. As she pressed the small child to her breast, bullets from his gun pierced her and her child, killing them both.

The Nazi occupiers did more than follow orders; they enjoyed exercising their license to kill. Every street and every field became a kill zone through which Halina had to navigate. She and her family could feel the terror stalking Warsaw. Each time they stepped into the street, they knew they might be experiencing the last minute of their lives.

It soon became clear the Polish people had some decisions to make. They could choose to resist and fight, be worked to death as slaves, or suffer slow strangulation behind the barbed wire of the concentration camps. The die was cast. The Poles would fight. The underground army and a variety of Resistance forces began to organize. The Union for Armed Struggle (ZWZ) was born. Later, in 1942, it was renamed the Polish Home Army. It answered to the legitimate Polish government in exile in London, England, and became a major force in the Resistance against the evil of the Third Reich.

～

It was almost like old times. Halina sat with a friend from the Girl Guides, and together they reminisced about happier days and all of the fun they had camping and playing in the woods. Later, five more guides entered the room. At this meeting, they were not there to play, as they did when children. Nor were they there to relive the past. The war was on, and they were well aware it would be a difficult, protracted affair. It was time to get down to business.

The discussion quickly moved to a question: How could they use their training as Girl Guides to assist the war effort? Already there was talk of the activities of the ZWZ. Fighting inevitably would mean casualties. Zophia, the young woman who owned the apartment where they were meeting, stood up to speak. "As I was walking on the roads, many kilometers to the east, I found people who were too slow to make it into the woods when the planes were strafing them. There was no reason for many of them to die. They were seriously wounded, sure. But there were no doctors in the group, and no one who knew what to do to stop the bleeding or bind their wounds."

Another girl spoke up. "But these were things we were taught to do when we were in the Guides."

"Precisely," Zophia replied. "That's why I asked you all to come here today. When the fighting begins in earnest, there will be a need for nurses to attend the wounded. We have these skills. I suggest we train girls to become nurses who can assist doctors in caring for the injured."

All agreed, and they devised a plan. Warsaw would be divided into five sectors. Each of the young women would be responsible to find and train volunteers and teach them basic nursing skills. Halina would be in charge of the Praga district. Her home was there, and she was familiar with many women in the area whom she thought would be ready to join the group.

Each girl in the room realized the gravity of the situation. Participating in the Resistance was a capital offense that would mean immediate execution if captured. For all practical purposes, these courageous young women were enlisting in the army that would fight the invaders over the next crucial years. About 1 million people lived in Warsaw. The ZWZ would draw its forces from those willing to put their lives on the line for their country and their beloved city on the Vistula. Before many days passed, a chief commandant was appointed. The fight against the Nazis, and later the Russians, was beginning in earnest. Halina was at war.

A Spiritual Pilgrimage

Halina had grown up in a Christian home and read the Bible. But the faith that sustained her through World War II was quite different from the faith she started out with. Her spiritual struggle began when she was nine years old and propelled her to the heights of bliss and the depths of despair.

The blissful times often were spent at the home of her English grandmother in Grochów, a suburb of Warsaw. Many years later, she described the experience:

> *I was very glad when my mother would take me to my Granny's, where I also saw my uncle and aunt. There was a garden, a playful dog, and time to run and play until we were worn out. During the day,*

when Granny rested on the sofa, she would show me pictures from a children's Bible. Her songs—I remember to this day—included "Gentle Jesus Meek and Mild," among many others.

She was also particular to teach me prayer: "Our Father who art in heaven . . ." It was because of her love for Jesus and stories about Him that I, too, began to love Him. What my dear Granny taught me in those happy days has never left me.

As the daughter of a teacher, Halina always had a love for books. When she turned nine, she developed a passion for reading the New Testament. It was a natural part of her development because her home had a shelf lined with family Bibles in a variety of languages. Some dated all the way back to her grandparents and even great-grandparents.

For her personal Bible, Halina chose a large New Testament with big print. It seemed easier to read and suited her capacity to absorb big ideas. Eager to share what she read, she often asked her mother's domestic helper to listen to her recite whatever passage captivated her attention. "Come," Halina would say. "Sit by me and listen."

The woman, who was Roman Catholic, resisted. "We are not allowed to read the Bible for ourselves without special permission from the priest," she told the child. "We are told that the Bible is a difficult book requiring special studies. It is not for average people like me. Average people go to church and listen to the sermons by the priests. That way we learn the teachings of our faith without being led astray."

Halina was not deterred. Her chance to make a listener out of her Mum's Roman Catholic helper came when Halina was sick with bronchitis, which meant long days in bed away from school with the woman sitting beside her administering medication. While the helper darned socks, Halina entertained her by reading from the New Testament, which her companion seemed to enjoy.

One day when she was alone, Halina came upon John 3:16: "For God so loved the world, that he gave his only begotten Son, that whosoever believeth in him should not perish, but have everlasting life."

> *I must have read the verse many times before. But that day I was struck that "God so loved the world" meant even me. And if He gave His only begotten Son to die for our sins, that meant everybody who believes should not perish, but have everlasting life.*
>
> *"Everlasting life" didn't mean only a long life, but life with God in heaven for all eternity.*

Halina became so excited at the prospect of receiving everlasting life that she got ready to jump from her bed to her knees and thank God for putting her sins on Jesus Christ. She was confident her father was enjoying eternal life. Immediately after he had died, three years earlier, her Granny entered Halina's room and sat on the edge of her bed. Taking Halusia in her arms, she told her, "You know child, your father is now in heaven."

"How wonderful!" thought the six-year-old. "I know that heaven is a marvelous place where there is joy and happiness. It is where Jesus lives with the angels and all of the people who loved God. Father will not suffer anymore. He is healthy. He is happy. He is in a beautiful place."

Her mother even confirmed that her father went to heaven. "The last words your father said were, 'Oh, what a beautiful garden.'"

Yet before Halina could get out of bed to thank God, a flood of distracting thoughts stopped her short. Her mind reeled with passages she had read where God severely condemned those who sinned. Though she was not a grievous sinner, she knew she sinned. When she contemplated the promise in the book of Revelation that Jesus will repay all sinners for their wicked deeds at His Second Coming, she gave up on the idea of bowing to thank Him for eternal life. Instead, she stayed in bed. She needed more information.

Leonardo da Vinci did not help her spiritual struggle. At age 14, Halina read a book about the life of the 15th-century painter, inventor, mathematician, and all-around icon. She loved reading about such towering figures who changed how people thought and acted, among them Socrates, Plato, Kant, and Nietzsche—none of whom were on the reading lists of the average teenaged girl.

It was a single comment attributed to da Vinci that hit her like a shock wave: "The truth is the daughter of time."

"If truth is the daughter of time," Halina reasoned, "then truth changes from one generation to another. Da Vinci may be right because people were at one time all pagans, praying to the sun, the moon, and who knows what. It was only later that Christianity came and changed religious beliefs. So if time changes truth, we may be wrong about what we believe. If he was right, then the Bible might be just a book of stories, myths, and legends."

The thought frightened her, causing her to doubt her faith and everything she had been taught about the Bible. Her prayers to God became anguished petitions for confirmation that truth does not change with time. "I believe there is a Creator who made the world, and He knows everything about all that goes on," she told herself. "Doesn't He tell the birds when it is time to fly south toward Egypt in the fall and when to come back to Poland when spring is coming? He must have plans. And if He has plans for animals, plants, and nature, He must have plans for human life. "Please, God," she prayed, "if we are wrong, and the truth is in another religion, show me; and I will change. If there is no truth to guide me, how will I find my way in life?"

In the depths of her struggle, she questioned her belief in Jesus, the truth of her faith, and the trustworthiness of the Bible. "If the truth changes with time, all my faith in the Bible and in Jesus Christ is meaningless. Could it be that everything I have learned to believe is merely a fable?"

Her torment grew until it became a giant specter that began dominating her life, throwing her into fits of restlessness at night until she no longer thought of herself as a Christian. Despite her doubts, she continued to cry out to God to show her the way. "Oh, God, help me," she would plead. "Oh, God, show me the truth, the real truth, and I will follow it." It would take more than two years before anything was settled.

The answer to her prayers appeared one day with the arrival in Warsaw of four missionaries from CMJ. They soon began holding services in English that Halina attended with her grandmother, aunt, and mother. Although she did not understand English well at the time, she saw something inspiring in their lives that set the people from CMJ apart from everyone else.

When Mr. Parsons spoke to the small congregation made up of business owners, staff members from the British Embassy, and a few Jewish believers in Jesus, she saw enthusiasm, love, and compassion in his eyes. Each missionary conveyed a sense of strength and optimism, even through difficulties. She could see a profound difference between their faith and what passed for faith among other people.

Miss Plinkington was a good example. The missionary was plagued by a persistent cough. Asked if it bothered her, she replied with a laugh, "Oh, no. My cough is an old friend."

Their cheerfulness and demeanor impressed Halina so much that she believed they could only behave the way they did because they were close to God. Only the Spirit of God could enable them to have such a consistently positive attitude.

Mr. Parsons' sermon particularly gripped her one day. Though she did not understand everything, she knew English well enough to get the gist of it. "Jesus is standing at the door of our hearts," he said. "And He wants to enter. But He cannot come in until we open the door." His words moved her to ask God to help her open the door of her heart to Jesus. But it was to no avail. As she left the building and walked into the street, doubts again overcame her; and the struggle for her soul intensified.

Fortunately, religious studies were compulsory for all students in pre-war Poland. They were required to bring to school a certificate from a clergyman, verifying their participation in religious training. To meet the requirement, her mother asked Rev. Jacob Yotch to oversee Halina's preparation. Before she arrived at the chapel for her first lesson, Halina had a conversation with herself. "If I am honest and tell him that I am not a believer, what will he say?" she thought. "Maybe he will not want to teach me, and he'll ask me to leave. But this would hurt Mother terribly, and where else could I go for lessons? It might be best if I don't tell him at all. But that would be dishonest, and I do not want to deceive him."

A torrent of conflicting thoughts ran through her mind as she entered the chapel. Inside she saw walls of books— floor to ceiling. Immediately she assumed Mr. Yotch was a very learned man. "Perhaps he has even read the books on philosophy that have caused me such doubts," she thought. To be on the safe side, she did not sit down but remained standing, close to the door. If he asked her to leave, she wouldn't be far from the exit.

Trembling, Halina got right to the point. "Sir, before we begin, I must tell you that I do not believe in God. That is to say, I almost completely believe there is no God. Rather, I should say that I have such doubts that I am not sure of my faith—or if I have any faith at all."

The jumble of words that tumbled from her mouth further confused her mind. When she finished talking, she waited for Mr. Yotch to order her out of the room. Instead, he invited her, "Come, sit down, and I'll tell you a secret." His voice was pleasant, and he didn't seem at all upset. "The secret is that I also was once an unbeliever," he said.

Halina breathed a huge sigh of relief. "At last," she thought, "I have found someone who understands what it means to be an unbeliever. Maybe he can help and stop the revolution inside of me."

Until now, her doubts had brought tears of anguish to her mother and expressions of pity from her relatives. No one seemed to know how to respond to her questions. But this man showed promise. Halina left the meeting with a feeling of camaraderie and the impression that Joseph Yotch may have the answers she sorely needed.

As things turned out, he proved to be a man of immense patience. His lessons were unlike anything Halina had encountered in the classroom. His teaching came directly from the Bible. If Mr. Yotch grew weary of hearing her say, "Yes, but," he never showed it. He concluded each weekly session on his knees with his pupil at his side, asking God to guide him and open her heart to His presence. The prayers became a powerful influence. Mr. Yotch prayed like a man with a strong personal attachment to the One he was addressing. Unlike many others she had heard pray, he prayed as though he were talking to someone he knew exceedingly well.

The lessons continued for nearly two years. Although Halina did not know it, all of the missionaries and members of the Warsaw congregation were praying that God would step in and make His presence known to her in a personal way.

๛

One warm autumn day, Halina was walking with Miss Plinkington in a park on Targowa Street. It was one of the most beautiful parks in Warsaw. That day it was teeming with people enjoying the warmth that preceded the soon-to-come chill of winter. Like everyone else, Halina and the missionary were taking advantage of the nice weather by strolling along the pleasant footpaths. Inevitably, their conversation turned to spiritual matters and Halina's constant quest for answers.

After an hour of chatting, Miss Plinkington excused herself, saying she had an appointment. She departed with a plea. "I have to go. And when you go home, remember the Lord Jesus Christ died for your sins. He died for you," she said. Then she added, "Go and thank Him."

The admonition "Go and thank Him" suddenly struck her as the antithesis of da Vinci's assertion, "Truth is the daughter of time." As Halina walked home, Miss Plinkington's words grew in intensity. "The Lord Jesus Christ died for you. Go and thank Him."

By the time she reached the stairs leading to the third

floor of her flat at 43 Targowa Street, the words were racing through her mind. She wanted desperately to fall to her knees and thank Him. But how? When she entered the flat, she discovered she was alone. Her brother and mother had gone out.

As she knelt down, she saw Jesus in her mind's eye. He seemed as real as if He were actually in the room with her. Still on the cross, with arms outstretched and beckoning her to come, His eyes were filled with compassion. Instead of rebuke and anger, she saw love. And that love was directed toward her. Suddenly, her resistance disappeared; and Halina prayed: "Lord, I should have been on that cross. I am a sinner. But you loved me so much that you were willing to go to that cross and die for me. I do believe. With all of my heart, I do believe. Now my life is no longer mine, but thine."

As she rose from her knees, the image faded. However, the assurance of His presence remained. Halina knew Christ was there, with her and in her. No longer did she need to search books for truth. Jesus was the truth, and the words of Scripture provided the message that would guide her life from then on. Thankfulness replaced doubt. The turmoil she had suffered intensely for two years was over, gone completely.

From that moment on, she would walk a new path. A new story would be written. And though she did not know what the future held, she was prepared to make the most of it. She now had a faith that was intensely personal—a vital, individual relationship with Jesus Christ. And it was that faith that sustained her when the Nazis took Poland.

CHAPTER 3

Heroes and Heroines

Though things in Poland were bad for everyone, they were worse for the Jewish people. The war against Poland's Jews began immediately following the German occupation, and the central arena for Hitler's "final solution" was Warsaw. Before the war, about 350,000 of the city's 1.3 million residents were Jewish. Warsaw not only had the largest Jewish population in Poland, but also in the whole of Europe. The only city with more Jews was New York City in the United States.

The Nazis wasted no time developing a blueprint to round up all the Jews and pack them into a confined area. Plans immediately were laid to build a wall around a portion of the city that would become the Warsaw Ghetto. All Jews were required to wear white armbands with a blue Star of David. The Nazis closed Jewish schools, confiscated Jewish property, and began corralling Jewish men into forced-labor camps.

By late October 1940, German authorities ordered all Jewish people in Warsaw and nearby towns to move to the Ghetto. More than 400,000 people were stuffed into an area slightly more than one square mile. Beyond the 10-foot brick and barbed-wire enclosure, heavily armed Nazi guards were posted to assure that passage in and out of the Ghetto was closely monitored or prevented altogether.

Jewish people were herded like cattle into the sector, where they lived nearly eight to a room. It was a prison. The captives, whose lives had been shattered, now merely existed, tormented each day by the premonition that the Ghetto would be their last stop on their journey to the grave.

At first, many Poles thought it might be good for the Jewish people to be in the Ghetto, however uncomfortable that may be. At least they would be somewhat safe from the vicious anti-Semitic attacks of recent years. That bubble of misplaced optimism soon burst. There were no safe havens from the Nazis—not for Jews and not for their former Polish neighbors.

With the Einsatzgruppen roaming the streets, the Poles soon learned they, too, were to be impaled on the spear of a well-planned crusade that would give them no more immunity than the Jews who were starving to death behind the Ghetto walls. All too common were long lines of Polish men standing against buildings with their hands raised and anguished looks on their faces. The crack of rifle shots filled the air; and the men toppled over like limp, inanimate objects.

One afternoon the young daughter of a Polish man was watching as her father was marched off with a group of men and lined up for the inevitable. Breaking away from the bystanders, she impulsively ran to the soldier in charge and pleaded for her father's life. "Please, sir, don't shoot my father. He is a good man who has done nothing wrong."

The officer replied gruffly, "Come here and open your impudent mouth."

Not knowing what to expect but hoping for a reprieve, she obeyed. As soon as she complied, the man put the barrel of his gun in her mouth and pulled the trigger. While she lay dead at his feet, the firing squad executed her father and all those standing with him.

Such atrocities became part of life under the Third Reich.

If you were not Aryan and a groveling believer in the neo-antichrist in Berlin, there was a place at the wall reserved for you.

Arbeit Macht Frei

It was obvious that Jewish people were not being penned up for their safety. They were being penned up to die. All they were allowed to carry into the Ghetto were small quantities of food. Everything else was left behind or confiscated as they entered the gates. Soon starvation and disease began to take their toll.

Halina and her friends knew that Hitler's *Mein Kampf*, written while he was in the Landsberg prison in 1924, declared his intentions. The twisted and sick ramblings of his deeply demented mind had become the official policy of the Third Reich. "It is the inexorable Jew," he wrote, "who struggles for his domination over the nations. No nation can remove this hand from its throat except by the sword. . . . Such a process is and remains a bloody one."

At the Klessheim conference in April 1943, Hitler spoke of the Jews in Poland. "If the Jews there don't want to work they will be shot. If they cannot work, they must rot. They should be treated like tubercular bacillus, which could attack healthy bodies. That is not cruel—if one keeps in mind that even innocent natural beings like hares and deer must be killed so that no damage occurs."

In the Warsaw Ghetto, Jewish people were indeed being left to rot. With overcrowded conditions, little food or medical care, and inadequate heat to protect them from the brutally cold winters, they soon began dying. Each morning emaciated bodies of people who had expired during the night lay out in the streets. Small carts, once used to carry vegetables, would clatter to a stop so that men could stack them full of bony corpses en route to a mass grave.

For those strong enough to work, there was Auschwitz, one of the Nazis' massive concentration camps that defaced the Polish countryside. Auschwitz was among the worst. Most of the people who went there never returned. Over the iron entrance gate were emblazoned the words *Arbeit Macht Frei* ("work makes one free"). They were a cruel mockery and deception, hiding the facility's true intent. The sign promised hope. The Nazis snidely referred to it as meaning "extermination through work."

Those selected for labor were systematically stripped of their clothing and all identification. After their heads were shaved, they stood in a line where each person received a blue tattoo on his or her forearm. It served as a registration number. Then they were issued the ragged garments and ill-fitting shoes that became their attire day and night.

By 1944, Auschwitz had become a complex of about 40 camps that processed at least 1.3 million people, 90 percent of them Jewish. Also deported to Auschwitz were 150,000 Poles and tens of thousands of people from other countries. At least 1.1 million died there, primarily in the gas chambers. Others died from starvation, forced labor, or disease.

Watching Germany's fierce, relentless determination to kill Jewish people paralyzed most of the Polish population. Associating with Jews in any way was an invitation to suffer the same fate. Sheltering or protecting someone Jewish was a capital offense punishable by execution. Yet, for those who would turn in someone Jewish, there was a reward: a bottle of vodka and 100 cigarettes. To the Germans, that was more than what a Jew was worth.

Some people refused to be intimidated. All over Nazi-occupied Europe there were courageous people willing to defy the Nazis. Some, out of a sense of compassion and outrage, sheltered, protected, and helped the Jews. Others, like Corrie ten Boom and her family, were born-again believers who willingly risked everything out of a deep, biblically motivated love for God's Chosen People.

Halina felt both compassion and a biblical motivation. She could never forget the faces of the malnourished Jewish boys she had seen as a little girl while on a shopping trip with her mother. Nor could she forget how Jewish people who had done no harm to anyone were shunned, ridiculed, and despised simply because they were different. She was moved by the intensity of the injustice and cruelty. And now they were wasting away in the Ghetto for no reason other than they were Jewish. The Ghetto children would never see a better world or experience a touch of compassion before they died hungry, beyond the reach of anyone who could help them.

For Halina and other members of the Resistance, the situation was intolerable. Even if it meant their lives, they were determined to use every means at their disposal to rescue as many people as they could from the hands of the Germans who had no concept of the sanctity of life.

〰

Dr. Janusz Korczak placed a high value on the sanctity of life. A well-known author and pediatrician, he ran a home for orphans in Warsaw and was determined to help as many Jewish children as he possibly could. During the war, he and his assistant of more than 30 years, Stefania Wilczynska, directed a staff that ministered to the needs of some 200 Jewish children ranging in age from two to 13.

In 1940 the Germans forced Dr. Korczak out of the

spacious orphanage he had designed and built and into the crowded quarters of the Warsaw Ghetto. Yet he and his small staff continued to teach the children, provide medical help for them, and keep up their morale despite the dismal surroundings.

The Zegota, an underground organization that aided Jewish people, offered to take Dr. Korczak to safety on the "Aryan side" of the city. He steadfastly refused. He would not abandon his children and was determined to stay with them, his devoted assistant, and a small group of nurses until the bitter end.

The beginning of the end showed up on August 5, 1942, in the person of an SS officer with orders for everyone, staff and children, to prepare for transfer to Treblinka. Located in the woods about 65 miles from Warsaw, Treblinka was not classed as a concentration camp. Rather, it was an "extermination" facility devoted entirely to liquidation. The process was simple: Victims were hustled off the trains and sent immediately to the gas chambers. Bodies were disposed of in a giant crematory built in the center of the site. Then they were dumped into mass, unmarked graves. It was a perverted tribute to a quality the Germans so highly prized: efficiency.

The facility operated between July 1942 and October 1943. In that brief time, it was used to murder more than 850,000 men, women, and children—800,000 of them Jewish.

People watched as Korczak's children left the Ghetto orphanage and began the march to the trains that would take them to Treblinka. Wearing their best clothing and carrying a favorite toy, the 200 children, walking four abreast, were quietly accompanied out of the Ghetto by the people who had loved them and cared for them and who stayed with them to the end. Mary Berg, an eyewitness, recorded this account in her book *The Diary of Mary Berg: Growing Up in the Warsaw Ghetto:*

> Dr. Janusz Korczak's children's home is empty now. A few days ago we all stood and watched the Germans surround the houses. Rows of children, holding each other by their little hands, began to walk out of the doorway. They were tiny tots of two or three years among them, while the oldest ones were perhaps thirteen. Each child carried the little bundle in his hand.[1]

Another survivor, who succeeded in escaping from the railroad platform, remembered what he saw as the doctor and the children were being loaded into the railroad cars:

> These children did not cry, these innocent little beings did not even weep. Like sick sparrows they snuggled up to their teacher, their caregiver, their father and their brother Janusz Korczak, that he might protect them with his weak, emaciated body.[2]

Today Dr. Korczak and his children are memorialized in bronze and stone figures that stand in Warsaw; at Yad Vashem, the Holocaust memorial in Jerusalem; and at a setting close to where the infamous crematory once stood at Treblinka.

తు

The Nazis did everything they could to hunt down Jewish people and kill them. Thanks to courageous Polish people who were willing to risk their lives to help them, a number of Jewish people survived.

A young Jewish girl named Miriam was hidden in a special hole dug beneath the kitchen floor. When Gestapo search parties were in the area, she would be lowered into the hiding place.

One day there was an ominous knock on the door. Outside a voice shouted the order, "Gestapo! Open up!" When the door swung open, the couple whose home it was found themselves staring into the stony faces of the capture squad and its large German Shepherd, which was trained to detect the scent of people even when they were concealed far out of sight.

Asked if there were any Jews on the premises, the couple answered no, certain they were only minutes away from being exposed. With them was their small dog, which they kept in the house as a pet. Unaccustomed to having a big German Shepherd around, the little dog became frightened.

As the Gestapo dog began the search, he was distracted by the scared little mutt who soon took one look at the open kitchen door, saw his way of escape, and bolted. As far as the search dog was concerned, the race was on. The Shepherd pulled away from his handler and headed for the open door. The Nazis quickly looked around and, not seeing anyone, left to find their dog. The couple then lifted Miriam from the hiding place. They had been saved by a mutt.

❧

Mr. Grinseit was being hidden by farmers. Their home was in a small village, and the only place they could find to conceal him was down a dry well. When the Gestapo came through the village hunting for Jewish people, Mr. Grinseit would slip into the well.

Thinking the well was the source of the farm's water supply, it never occurred to the Nazis to look down the shaft. When they left and the farmers saw it was safe again, they would retrieve Mr. Grinseit, take him back into the house, and see that he got warm again and had something to eat. Amazingly, this system continued throughout all the years of the war until the area was liberated by the Russians.

℘

Some Jewish families tried to flee the cities for the country, where they thought it would be easier to hide. One such family had a 14-year-old daughter. With the help of friends, they were introduced to people who placed Jews with peasant farmers in an attempt to save their lives.

The decision was made that this family should be divided. The father and mother went to a farm with only enough room for the two of them. The daughter was hidden in another village some distance away in, of all places, a pigsty. The pigs were long gone, and there was plenty of hay available to provide some degree of comfort and warmth.

As one would expect, the girl missed her parents terribly. When her longing for them became more than she could bear, she left her hiding place and went to see them. On the way back, she was spotted by a group of Polish boys who recognized her Jewish features, followed her, and began to shout, "Jude! Jude!" meaning "Jew! Jew!"

Trembling with fear, she began to run from them. But where could she go? If she ran to the farm where she was being protected, she would expose the people protecting her and lead to their execution.

The answer came when she was running past an intersection in the road where a large cross stood—a common sight in Poland in those days. In a moment of desperation, she stopped before the cross, lifted both her arms, and began to cry out, "Jesus! Jesus! Help me!" When the boys saw what she was doing, they thought they had made a mistake in thinking her Jewish. So they stop chasing her, and she was able to return to the pigsty.

When she was safe, she began thinking about her ordeal. She had called out to Jesus, and even the sound of His name had caused the boys to let her go. The name of Jesus probably had saved her from death. Yet all through her life she had been told never to speak His name because, since the Middle Ages, "Christian" churches had been at the forefront of Jewish persecution. In fact, many Jewish people even referred to Jesus as "the great anti-Semite."

She asked herself, "Have I committed a great sin by calling on His name?" In her anguish, she called out to the God of Abraham, Isaac, and Jacob, asking for forgiveness if what she had done was wrong.

The rest of her story was related to Halina in Israel after the war. The young woman had become a believer in Jesus as her Savior and Israel's Messiah and told Halina at a convent where the woman lived as a nun.

ℕ

Another brave Gentile couple lived in a suburb of Warsaw with their 10-year-old daughter, Marianna. Also in the house was a guest—a Jewish man they were concealing from the Nazis.

Their home was not conducive to building a hidden room where he could flee in case of a raid. The hiding place they devised was a stroke of ingenuity but also a place of close confinement. In the basement was a coal bin used to store fuel in the winter. Using boards, they built a box large enough for the man to sit in, then covered it with coal. When the Gestapo was in the area, the man got in the box and stayed there until he was told it was safe to come out.

Although the hiding place was clever, it was extremely uncomfortable. The man was confined for hours to the pitch-black interior, which was an invitation to claustrophobia and suffocation. The dire need for fresh air proved the undoing of others who took unnecessary chances to emerge from their hiding places for a bit of relief.

One day the man felt he had to get out and walk. It was dangerous, but he had done it before and felt he would not be in imminent danger of capture. This time he was wrong. He had reached a roundabout (traffic circle) where people were gathered, waiting to cross the street. Suddenly, uniformed Germans surrounded them and ordered them to stay put until trucks came to pick up every person able to work.

When Marianna came home from her school operated by the Resistance, her first question was, "Where is Uncle?"

"He's gone out for a walk. He's probably in the park," said her mother.

Marianna immediately shouted to her mother, "There is a *lapanka!*" meaning a roundup of people to be sent to labor camps. Impulsively, the girl dashed out of the house and was soon at the roundabout where at least 100 people were standing. Walking boldly past the German police, she slipped through the crowd hoping to find her "uncle." When she spotted him, she ran to him and leaped into his arms.

"Uncle, come. We've all been waiting for you at home." Slowly, slowly the Jewish man holding the child in his arms started toward the house. Miraculously, the two of them walked passed the armed Gestapo guards, who made no effort to stop them.

After discussing the "miracle escape," the family concluded the only reason they both made it was because little Marianna was being carried with her arms around the neck of her "uncle," who from then on would be more cautious and remain safe until the end of the war. After the war, the family was awarded a medal from the State of Israel for being "righteous among the nations."

৵

Rozalia and her husband lived in Kraków. They were social people and had many Jewish friends. Rozalia was deeply disturbed when she went to visit some of them one day and learned they had all been taken to the Kraków Ghetto. Food in the Ghetto was scarce, and people were dying of starvation.

Because Kraków was the headquarters of Gen. Hans Frank, Hitler's governor-general for all of Poland, the city had electricity. That meant that, unlike in Warsaw, the trams were operating. Each day a tram passed through the Ghetto without stopping and later made a return trip using the same route.

Rozalia worked out a dangerous plan to jump off the tram when it slowed nearly to a stop as it made a particularly sharp turn. Fortunately, the spot was outside the line of vision of the German Ghetto guards. Almost every day she boarded the tram, jumped off, saw her friends, and jumped back on.

On every trip, she brought a bag full of loaves of bread provided free by a local baker. Once inside the Ghetto, Rozalia immediately went to see her friends, checked on their condition, and delivered the bread that enabled them to survive. Her friends also shared it with others. The visits were short because every time Rozalia jumped off the tram to walk through the Ghetto, she was in great danger. If caught, her compassionate ministry to her Jewish friends would have ended with her death.

✍

Later in life, Halina recounted a story she heard from the wife of a courageous man named Adam. Because he was a specialist in a trade the Germans needed, Adam was given a pass to go in and out of the Ghetto. Every day he would go in and work in a shop. Because he could move about freely, he became proficient in smuggling Jewish people out past the guards.

One day a woman approached him, frantic to save her newborn from starvation and death. "Okay," he said. "Bring the baby to me, and I'll see what I can do."

He placed the infant in his tool satchel and held his breath as he walked out past the guards. He knew if the child cried or made a sound, it would be the end of them both. Fortunately, the child slept the entire time. So with the child in his bag, he walked out of the Ghetto and back to his home.

Later Adam was also able to smuggle the mother out and reunite her with her child. Thirty years later, Halina met the satchel baby, by then a successful engineer. Throughout the war, Adam and his wife continued to provide temporary shelter for many Jewish people in their one-room apartment. Had the Gestapo gotten wind of what they were doing, it would have rewarded the couples' heroism with execution.

✍

One of the most well-known heroines was Irena Sendler, who risked her life to smuggle 2,500 Jewish children out of the Warsaw Ghetto. She provided them with false documents and placed them with families and organizations on the outside.

Such was life in Poland under the Nazi reign of terror.

The extreme cruelty and inhumanity of Germany's so-called best and brightest caused some to rethink their belief that an inherent "spark of goodness" dwells within everyone. They saw no "spark" in Hitler's Nazis.

Innocent blood filled the streets, put there happily by men who considered themselves superior to the rest of humanity. Being Polish in the Third Reich meant either giving in to death or battling to survive. Halina chose the latter.

---

[1] Mary Berg, *The Diary of Mary Berg: Growing Up in the Warsaw Ghetto* (Oxford: Oneworld Publications, 1996), 169–170.

[2] Wolfgang Hergeth, *Janusz Korczak's Biography,* University of Minnesota Center for Holocaust and Genocide Studies <chgs.umn.edu/museum/responses/hergeth/bio.html>.

CHAPTER 4

Living at the Gates of Hell

Halina was a soldier in the Polish Home Army, which led the Resistance. Though there were no uniforms, she was issued a red and white armband—the colors of the flag of Poland. Serving in the Resistance meant living moment by moment. Each day, Halina and her Girl Guide friends demonstrated uncompromising courage and a willingness to make great sacrifices for others and for the hope of freedom. Eluding capture meant life, at least temporarily. Getting captured usually meant death.

Halina's group, along with others in the Home Army, was in a race to rescue as many Jewish people as possible before Hitler succeeded in exterminating them all. The Polish underground reportedly saved more Jewish lives during the Holocaust than any other organization or government.

Though Jewish people fared the worst, Christians were in no way exempt from Hitler's plan. Nazi ideology directly conflicted with Christian theology. Wherever anti-Semitism rages, defiance toward God emerges. In Hitler's scheme of things, the Third Reich was the new millennium—destined to last one thousand years. *Mein Kampf* was the Bible for the new order, and the Führer himself was the new Messiah. A prayer recited in all orphanages under Nazi control reflected the heresy:

Leader, my Leader, given to me by God, protect me and sustain my life for a long time. You have rescued Germany out of deepest misery. To you I owe my daily bread. Leader, my Leader, my belief, my light. Leader my Leader, do not abandon me.

In prewar Poland, the vast majority of the people were Roman Catholic. It quickly became evident that Nazi fanaticism and devout Catholicism did not mix. Although there were rare exceptions, the Germans shut down monasteries, convents, schools, seminaries, and other institutions operated by the Roman Catholic Church.

In many areas not only were the churches closed, but the majority of priests were killed, imprisoned, or deported. It has been estimated that between 1939 and 1945, 3,000 Catholic clergy were executed. Hundreds of nuns were sent to concentration camps.

Protestant churches fared no better. In one area alone, all members of the Protestant clergy were arrested and sent to death camps. Across the country, thousands of other clergymen were imprisoned or killed. The Christian faith was incompatible with Nazi dogma. Christians worshiped God. The Nazis worshiped Hitler. Reconciliation was impossible.

Because pastors were often community leaders, they became prime targets for extermination. Protestant ministers were forced into concentration camps, along with the priests. Their combined numbers totaled in the thousands. Few survived. Many were executed. Most were consigned to a slow and torturous death by starvation or sickness.

In Warsaw the situation worsened by the day. A diary entry written in 1941 lamented, "The most fearful sight is that of freezing children" who stand "dumbly weeping in the street with bare feet, bare knees, and torn clothing."[1]

The city lay virtually in ruins. The Jews were penned up like animals. Every place that could provide work lay in German hands, and the only people who could obtain food were those who had documents bearing the insignia of the German eagle.

Fortunately, Halina had such a document because she managed to get work in a plant that packed fruit for the German army. But she still struggled to find enough for her mother and her to eat. The Nazis only gave preferential treatment to people who could prove they were German or had German ancestry. For the average Pole, there was only a meager distribution each week of unwholesome, wheatless bread and a bit of margarine—hardly enough to sustain life.

The only option was to leave the city and venture into the country to buy food from peasant farmers. But it was a dangerous enterprise. Both the buyer and seller could be killed if caught. But Halina had no choice. It was a risk she had to take. From time to time she left Warsaw to buy whatever she could from the villagers. Often she returned home with a rucksack filled with lard, eggs, bread, and other life-sustaining supplies. She knew she had to be careful. Her Girl Guide skills were put to good use as she kept a close lookout for the Gestapo, which watched diligently for offenders.

The peasant women watched for the Gestapo too. Despite the danger, they came from the villages into the city with food concealed in blankets or under their clothes to help the people of Warsaw. If they were caught, they were severely beaten, and the precious commodity they risked their lives to bring in was wasted. If they brought milk, the Nazis poured it out on the ground. If they brought bread or meat or eggs or anything else, the Nazis confiscated it and made sure the women returned home bloodied and empty-handed. Yet they kept running the gauntlet to bring life-saving supplies into the city. Some say these brave women were the salvation of the starving people of Warsaw.

Helping the starving Jews were the courageous child merchants. They dug potatoes from the fields and smuggled them into the Ghetto, often crawling through the slimy sewers to get inside the wall, then crawling back out again.

The new Poland was a world of darkness, devastation, and death—a perpetual nightmare. Adding to Halina's stress was her separation from her brother, Zygmund. Since the war broke out, she had no knowledge of his whereabouts and only had bits of information about her many other relatives. How many had been killed? She had no idea. Already there had been news of the death of a cousin who was an engineer. He was arrested as an undesirable, taken to Auschwitz, and tortured until he died.

The difficult circumstances become especially hard on Halina's mother, who had never enjoyed robust health. She could see her mum wither as the war and its uncertainties weighed on her.

Halina wondered what would happen to the two of them. Millions of others throughout Europe were asking themselves the same question. Poland's future looked bleak, to say the least. Reality and hope seemed like disparate entities separated by an unbridgeable chasm. Hitler was well on his way to eliminating the nation altogether and repopulating it with Germanic Aryan stock. German-occupied Poland housed 430 complexes specially built for specific Nazi operations, including extermination camps, concentration camps, labor camps, and prisoner of war camps. Each day smoke from the crematories fouled the Polish air as thousands of Jewish bodies went up in flames.

People could not even walk the streets. If men were out at an inopportune moment, when the Gestapo was rounding up every able body, they were captured, thrown into trucks, and hauled away as slaves to be worked until they died.

The whole of Poland had become a prison, and the country

was literally starving to death. The quest for heat and light was perpetual, and staying alive became the universal objective.

The Warsaw Ghetto Uprising

For the Jews in the Warsaw Ghetto, life went from bad to worse. The Germans were systematically tightening a proverbial noose around their necks, hoping they would die. Starvation, among other things, was killing thousands, but not fast enough to suit the Nazis.

The food rations provided by the German civilian authorities in 1941 were not sufficient to sustain life. The smugglers were helping a little with what they could bring in, but they could not reverse the conditions of severe deprivation, malnutrition, and sickness. Had it not been for their brave efforts, however, the death toll would have risen more quickly.

Between 1940 and mid-1942, an estimated 83,000 people in the Ghetto succumbed to starvation and disease. Hitler had a plan; and no matter how long it took or how sinister the means, he was determined to rid the world of European Jewry.

In all areas under German occupation, the Jewish people were "represented" by a *Judenrat* (German for "Jewish Council"), which the Nazis compelled them to form. In Warsaw, Adam Czerniaków held a position on the council. He, like others appointed by the Nazis, entertained the view that cooperating would lessen the severity of the occupation and eventually facilitate the survival of a significant number of his brethren. Instead, as matters worsened, *Judenrat* leaders were generally seen as collaborators with the enemy.

Adam Czerniaków was an exception. When he received

orders from the SS to provide a quota of 6,000 Jews a day, including children, for deportation to the death camps, he was sickened. In a letter to his wife, Czerniaków wrote, "They are asking me to participate in the murder of the children of my people. I have no other choice but to die."

True to his word, the leader of the Warsaw Jewish Council killed himself. On the same day he committed suicide, the newly opened extermination camp at Treblinka snuffed out the lives of everyone who had been on the first transport from the Warsaw Ghetto. By September 1942, more than 250,000 Jews from the Ghetto had been murdered at Treblinka.

Czerniaków's determination to choose death over complicity in the slaughter of his people was a harbinger of things to come. Another decision was being made among the remaining Ghetto residents. Every day trucks pulled up empty, and then left filled past capacity with scared, broken human beings who were being deported to certain death. So if death was inevitable, why not die fighting? Thus began preparations for the Warsaw Ghetto uprising.

In 1942 Hitler decided all ghettos would be liquidated and all Jews who had somehow survived would be sent to extermination camps to be murdered by bullets or gas. The Nazis preferred gas because bullets were too expensive and inefficient. They then dumped the bodies into mass graves or burned them in crematories. Wrote foreign policy expert Mitchell Bard, director of the Jewish Virtual Library,

> The Germans ordered the Jewish "police" in the Warsaw ghetto to round up people for deportation. Approximately 300,000 men, women, and children were packed in cattle cars and transported to the Treblinka death camp where they were murdered. This left a Jewish population of between 55,000 and 60,000 in the ghetto.[2]

Some Jewish people felt if they tried to fight, perhaps they might survive. Preparations for the uprising were primitive. After a slight skirmish in January 1943 that surprised the Germans into withdrawing from the Ghetto, people began preparing to do battle. The previous confrontation had encouraged the Jews somewhat, giving them a slight hope that the Nazis might think twice before again attempting to deport them for extermination. The SS, meanwhile, was concerned that Jewish resistance would inspire Polish Gentiles in Warsaw to rise up and fight as well. So the SS was all the more determined to squelch any stand the Jews might take, and to squelch it viciously.

Between January and mid-April, Jewish leaders in the Ghetto mapped out plans for resistance. They constructed makeshift bunkers in the basements of buildings for protection and as places of refuge where they could sustain life when the Germans began to retaliate. The headquarters for the operation was the bunker at Mila 18, underneath the building at 18 Mila Street.

Led by 23-year-old Mordecai Anielewicz, the Ghetto fighters organized under the banner of Zydowska Organizacja Bojowa (ZOB), Polish for "Jewish Fighting Organization." They didn't have much to fight with. Weapons were in pitifully short supply. According to reports, approximately 750 courageous Jews, armed with a small number of pistols, 17 rifles, and Molotov cocktails, confronted 2,000 heavily armed, well-trained German troops supported by tanks and flamethrowers.[3] By anyone's standards, they did not stand a chance.

As the final deportation orders were issued, the Germans called their troops into action. To do the job, Heinrich Himmler appointed Jürgen Stroop, a 47-year-old, high-ranking Nazi who embraced neo-paganism and had as little use for Christians as he did for Jews. He spoke of the "rottenness" of the Judeo-Christian ethic. A man with a wealth of experience in fighting partisans, Stroop was given the task of executing the final deportations and dismantling the Warsaw Ghetto. When the Germans attempted to round up the Jews for the trip to the death camps, the conflict began in earnest.

Shortly before the trucks arrived, Jewish fighters received word that the final deportation was about to begin. As the pickup trucks rolled into the Ghetto, the Nazis anticipated herding their victims together and shoving them onto the vehicles, as they had done many times before. Instead, they met resistance.

The Jewish people were so emaciated and ill-equipped that the fight should have ended quickly. Yet it raged on for an astonishing 27 days. Frustrated by his inability to finish off his victims, Stroop issued orders to kill them by burning down the Ghetto, one building at a time.

With nowhere to go, families huddled together in the underground bunkers as the young Jews fought courageously, street by street and building by building. It seemed as though they were reliving the history of their ancient forefathers who made their famous yet fatal last stand against the Romans at Masada in the Judean wilderness in the first century. The Jews of the Warsaw Ghetto were in the grips of a hopeless struggle. They could never win. But their selfless heroism, even in defeat, lives on.

For those who were on the outside looking in, the sights and sounds were forever imprinted in their memories. The recollections of some have been recorded by the U.S. Holocaust Memorial Museum in Washington, DC. Here are two accounts from people who spoke many years later about what they witnessed:

Vladka Peltel Meed. Vladka belonged to the Zukunft youth movement of the Bund (the Jewish Socialist party). She was active in the Warsaw Ghetto underground as a member of the ZOB. According to the U.S. Holocaust Memorial Museum, "In December 1942, she was smuggled out to the Aryan, Polish side of Warsaw to try to obtain arms and find hiding places for children and adults. She became an active courier for the Jewish underground and for Jews in camps, forests, and other ghettos."[4]

> While being there at night, I saw the flames of the ghetto. And I saw also certain pictures which were seared in my mind. Some Jews running from one place to the other and also seeing some Jews jumping from buildings, but I was observing this from a window and I couldn't do anything. . . . [When] the Germans couldn't take over the streets, they started putting block after block on fire. They started burning the ghettos . . . the buildings, and this was the uprising which we . . . the small group on the Aryan side, we tried to get through. We tried to communicate. We decided even to go into the ghetto to be with them but it was, everything was in vain. We didn't have any communication. We saw only tanks coming in, tanks going out, or some ambulances going in and we're listening to the shooting, and in that time . . . [we said to one another] we have to let the outside know what is going on.[5]

Benjamin Meed. Ben was one of four children born to a religious Jewish family. After the Germans occupied Warsaw in September 1939, he escaped to Soviet-occupied eastern Poland. However, he soon decided to return to his family, all of whom were in the Warsaw Ghetto. Ben was assigned to a work detail outside the Ghetto and helped smuggle people out. One of the women he rescued was Vladka (Fagele)

Peltel, a ZOB member who later became his wife.

Eventually, he went into hiding on the outside, posing as a Polish Gentile. During the uprising in 1943, Ben worked with other members of the underground to rescue Ghetto fighters, bringing them out through the sewers and hiding them on the Aryan side of Warsaw. From the Aryan side, Ben witnessed the Ghetto going up in flames. After the uprising, he escaped from Warsaw by passing as a Gentile. Following the liberation, he was reunited with his father, mother, and younger sister.[6] Here is what he saw:

> The entire sky of Warsaw was red. Completely red. But the flames were so concentrated around the whole ghetto that it illuminate[d] the whole city. The next week, the same week was Palm Sunday. I couldn't be anymore in the [ghetto] with my parents. . . . I walked out on that Palm Sunday and I went to Plac Krasinski where there was a church, a very old church, and I felt that my safest place is in the church. I went to that church and I attended the Mass and the priest spoke. Not a word was mentioned that across the street people are fighting, dying by the hundreds. . . . I was just like a good Christian listening to the whole sermon. Then it is, uh, traditional in Poland that, . . . after the services, the priest goes out in front of the church and he greets the parish . . . the people. [This is probably] practiced in every country the same way, but in Poland it is a traditional thing. . . . Across the street was a carousel with a playground and the music was playing. [Some] people took the children to ride on the carousel. . . . I was standing in that group watching the other side of the block, of that burning ghetto. From time to time we heard screaming, "Look. Look. People are jumping from the roofs." Others will make remarks, uh, "Jews are

frying." That's just a free translation from Polish. But I never heard any sympathy voices. Maybe there were people who looked in a different way, but I never heard it. And it was very heartbreaking for me that here I am, helpless, I can do nothing, and I gotta see and watch, and I cannot even protest, I cannot even show my anger. Sometimes I felt . . . that I have to do something physically, even have to pay with my life, start screaming, but I didn't do it. I didn't scream. I didn't do anything. I just was hurt. But that scene will probably remain with me for all my life.[7]

Witnessing the terrifying scene were Halina and her fellow soldiers in the Polish Home Army. Appalled and frustrated, they watched helplessly as the Ghetto and its innocent Jewish people went up in flames. "Why can't we do something to help them?" she asked her commanding officer.

The officer replied sadly, "With what? We do not have armaments. We have to wait for our allies to come and supply us. Then we can help, and we can fight."

They waited, but no help came. For the Jews of the Ghetto, it was too late. Halina later told her friends, "It was a terrible sight to see. Night after night, we saw the flames and the red sky over the Ghetto, knowing that people were dying. And we could do nothing for them. . . . It was really terrible for those of us who loved the Jews and who would have tried to help them." Wrote Holocaust scholar Lucy S. Dawidowicz,

> The ghetto was a roaring sea of fire. ZOB fighters regrouped their forces and began rescuing the Jews in the shelters, where thousands were being burned alive. People were seen silhouetted in the window frames of blazing buildings, sheathed in flames, like living torches.[8]

On May 16, 1943, Jürgen Stroop announced that the fighting was over. He declared that as a symbol of their victory, the Nazis would blow up the Great Synagogue on Tlomackie Street, located outside the Ghetto. It would be a dramatic witness to the fact the Jewish quarter of Warsaw was gone. In triumph, he sent the following message to the SS Command:

> 180 Jews, bandits and subhumans were destroyed. The Jewish quarter of Warsaw is no more! The grand operation terminated at 2015 hours when the Warsaw synagogue was blown up. . . . The total number of Jews apprehended and destroyed, according to the record, 56,065.[9]

The apprehended were carted off to Treblinka. Wrote Mitchell Bard, "The outcome was preordained, but the dramatic act of resistance helped raise the morale of Jews everywhere, if only briefly."[10] The country's Jewish society was obliterated. Dawidowicz gave the following account:

> Every day the number of surviving Jews dwindled. In the cities, Polish police, blackmailers, spies, Gestapo agents, and Security Police hunted down Jews, especially Jewish leaders. In the forest, unfriendly peasants and anti-Semitic Polish, Ukrainian, or Russian partisans found it easier to destroy Jews than Germans. As for the labor camps and the camps at Vittel and Bergen-Belsen, the Germans liquidated them in rapid order.[11]

For the most part, the number of Jewish people left who were not in labor or extermination camps were in hiding; and even their numbers were dwindling: "There were no Jewish communities anymore, no synagogues, no Jewish schools, no Jewish life to sustain. Blood-soaked debris of Yiddish and Hebrew books at the banks of the Vistula were all that remained of the thousand-year-old civilization of Jews in Poland."[12]

[1] Lucy S. Dawidowicz, *The War Against the Jews 1933–1945*, 10th anniversary ed., introduction by Lucy S. Dawidowicz (New York, NY: Bantam Books, 1976), 209.

[2] Mitchell Bard, "Warsaw Ghetto Uprising," Jewish Virtual Library <jewishvirtuallibrary.org/jsource/Holocaust/uprising1.html>.

[3] Ibid.

[4] Vladka (Fagele) Peltel Meed, "Warsaw Ghetto Uprising— Oral History," United States Holocaust Memorial Museum <ushmm.org/wlc/en/media_oi.php?ModuleId=10005188&MediaId=1228>.

[5] Ibid.

[6] Benjamin Meed, "Warsaw Ghetto Uprising—Oral History," United States Holocaust Memorial Museum <ushmm.org/wlc/en/media_oi.php?ModuleId=10005188&MediaId=1096>.

[7] Ibid.

[8] Dawidowicz, 340.

[9] *The Stroop Report*, trans. Sybil Milton, introduction Andrzej Wirth (New York, NY: Pantheon, 1979), May 16, 1943.

[10] Bard.

[11] Dawidowicz, 340.

[12] Ibid.

CHAPTER 5

The Warsaw Insurrection

As the war dragged on, the Polish fighters were beginning to tire of living on promises that never materialized. Rumors abounded that hostilities would end in a few months and the Allies would come to their aid with airlifts of weapons and supplies. But that did not happen.

The Germans controlled most of Warsaw, and food was scarce. At first, people had what they squirreled away in anticipation of a siege. Halina and her fellow soldiers could count on at least one meal a day of kasha soup. But then the food supply dwindled, and finding something to eat became much more difficult.

One day as Halina was cleaning up after a sparse meal of tomato soup, she gained insight on how little the outside world really knew about what was going on in Poland. She had shared the soup with a soldier from England who was dropped in behind enemy lines. Dismayed that the utensils were not being washed, only scraped off and wiped with a rag, he asked Halina, "Why do you not wash these dishes properly? Aren't you aware that serious health problems can be caused by this?"

"You see," said Halina as she continued to wipe, "we have little water—only some for drinking. The Germans have cut off water to the city, and so we make do the best we can."

It was then she realized how little information about their dire circumstances had made it to the Allies. Later, that incident and other information she received forced her to conclude the troops in the Polish Home Army had been left to fight on their own. At least for the time being, they could expect little help from others, who were occupied with their own problems.

∽

The burden of being mostly alone was beginning to take its toll on Halina. Occasionally, some small act of defiant patriotism temporarily lifted her spirits. When she saw anchors shaped like the letters "P" and "W" on a wall in chalk or black paint, she knew they had been put there by boys or girls from the Scouting movement who were risking their lives to encourage their countrymen. The Scouts knew the price they would pay if caught. "P" stood for Poland and "W" for *walczy*, meaning "fighting." Together, the message was "Poland is fighting." To Halina and her friends in the Resistance, the words sparked the hope that someday the winter of war would be over and Poland would somehow make it through.

Unfortunately, there was more to discourage her than encourage her. Halina received news from the north of Warsaw where her mother and family were living. Their neighborhood had come under total Nazi control. Halina was now completely cut off from everyone she loved. Surrounded daily by the carnage of battle, she began to wonder if she would ever see her family again. As she moved daily between the flames of burning structures bombed by the Luftwaffe and the foul stench of death, she began to lose faith that there would ever be a successful end to the war.

Then a consuming thought entered her mind. "Why am I alive when so many around me have been killed? Am I better than they? What sins have they committed that I have not committed that has earned death for them and allowed me to escape?"

It was the same type of question she had been asking herself ever since she had returned home from a visit to the dentist when she was 12 years old. While she sat in the dental chair, the dentist told her of a homicide she had read about in the newspaper. A mother had been found guilty of murdering her own child. Obviously upset, the dentist related the story in lengthy detail. Halina became so profoundly preoccupied with it that she couldn't sleep.

"Why aren't you asleep, child?" her mother asked when she looked in on her.

"Because when I was at the dentist's office today, she told me a story that I cannot get out of my mind." She then related the details.

"Well, it is a terrible story; and she should not have told it to you. There must have been something terribly wrong with the mother's mind to prompt her to do such a thing to her own child. I can tell you that such a thing could never happen to you. You are God's child. He is watching over you. I'll get my Bible and show you why I can say this." Halina's mum quickly returned to the room with the Bible opened to Psalm 91. Slowly, she read the entire passage, which speaks about the protection God promises to His people.

> He that dwelleth in the secret place of the Most High shall abide under the shadow of the Almighty. I will say of the LORD, He is my refuge and my fortress: my God; in him will I trust. . . . A thousand shall fall at thy side, and ten thousand at thy right hand; but it shall not come nigh thee. . . . For he shall give his angels charge over thee, to keep thee in all thy ways. They shall bear thee up in their hands (vv. 1–2, 7, 11–12).

After her mother tucked her in, turned off the light, and

left the room, Halina lay awake, going over the words of the psalm in her mind.

"But how can I believe this?" she asked herself? "How is it possible that one thousand people may fall, be killed or wounded, and somebody can still be alive? Why wouldn't I be among the thousands who fell, rather than the one who escaped death?" That question had never been answered to her satisfaction.

These troubling thoughts seemed to have merit in her current state of mind. All she could think about were instances where she had escaped death when those around her had not. A round from a tank had killed someone walking directly in front of her, and she was untouched. A man and a woman between whom she was standing were both hit by a bomb and gunfire, and she was unhurt. In an instant, the woman stood with half of her face shot away, while the man lay writhing on the ground, both of his legs blown off.

Such thoughts plagued Halina, sending her into a severe depression. One day she left the underground hideout she shared with Resistance fighters and sat alone in the darkness. "Maybe," she thought, "it would be better if I ended it all myself, here and now. It would be better than going on without enough weapons or food and with no hope of this ordeal ending without being killed like the others."

Distraught and almost in a daze, she decided to end her life. The only weapon she had was a knife. With guns in such short supply, a knife was all a fighter was issued. As she began to take measures to accomplish the deed, she became conscious of a deep spiritual darkness. Though she had thought of her loved ones, she had given no thought to God. She had forgotten the Savior.

But He had not forgotten her. Suddenly, in her mind's

eye, Halina found herself wrapped in a light as bright as a brilliant sunrise. Then she became aware of someone in the light. She was convinced the Person was the Lord. And though she didn't actually see Him, she was certain of His presence. Then His voice seemed to invade her mind and repeat words she had said when she was only 16: "My life is not mine, it is Thine."

Then the words came back to her, "Your life is not yours. It is Mine."

Suddenly, Halina was awakened by the realization of what she was trying to do. She knew the Lord had not forgotten that she had promised to serve Him, and He was there to save her from herself. Engulfed in a torrent of inner pain, she burst into a prayer of commitment: "Dear Lord, my beloved Savior, please forgive me. I am so ashamed. Please, Lord, give me understanding of what is right and what is not. Let me not sin against Thee. Let me understand Thy will. Teach me Thy will, that I do not make mistakes. I want to follow Thee. I want always to remember that my life is not mine. It is Thine."

During the traumatic encounter in the midst of a cruel and bloody war, this child of God learned something of great value. She would never fully understand why she was still alive while thousands around her were dying. But it became overwhelmingly important to her to accept the fact that, whether she understood it or not, God had plans for her future. And until His plans were complete, she would live.

After spending a long time alone, pondering what had happened and what she had learned about herself and her imperishable relationship to her Savior, Halina was His. Never again would she question or forget that fact. With a peace that had previously eluded her, she slipped back into the shelter and fell sleep.

∽

The year that passed after the Warsaw Ghetto uprising exacted a heavy toll on Halina, both physically and emotionally. The daily struggle against the Germans and the torment of watching helplessly as the Ghetto burned became more stress than she could handle.

About one month after the Ghetto's destruction, Halina found herself slipping out of consciousness. Her head was bursting with pain, and she knew something was desperately wrong. At only 24, she was in the throes of a debilitating stroke. When she regained consciousness, the army doctors attending her gave her the bad news. "You have had a serious stroke that has impaired your ability to walk, and we cannot be certain how this will turn out. What we know now is that you must have a complete rest away from the work of the Resistance."

For one so totally committed to the war effort, the diagnosis was devastating. Even worse was the uncertainty of whether she would ever be well enough to help battle the Nazis who had destroyed her country.

It was an immense relief when she started to regain some strength in her legs and take the few small steps that began the long process of rehabilitation. It would be nearly a full year before she was able to resume her duties as a lieutenant in the Home Army. Her reentry into active service came none too soon. Within the month, the Resistance began a heroic struggle against insurmountable odds to drive the Nazis out.

From 1939 to 1945, the only viable options for the Polish people were to flee or fight. For most, fleeing was impossible. And though fighting seemed a hopeless folly, it was worth a try. Whether due to bravado or overconfidence, the Polish Resistance was overly optimistic about how soon the war would end. Gen. Tadeusz Bór-Komorowski, commander of the Polish Home Army, timed an uprising for August 1, 1944. He speculated the fighting would be over in two days or a week at most, an estimate based partly on the supply of weapons available.

He was wrong. Neither he nor anyone on his staff was aware the Nazis had decided to defend Warsaw. They intended to make a stand that would buoy up the spirits of Germans who were beginning to despair over the Allied forces' June invasion of France and Germany's losses to the Russians in the East.

The German garrison contained about 15,000 soldiers. On the surface, the Poles seemed to outnumber the Nazis. They had some 40,000 insurgents, including Halina and 4,000 other women, and counted heavily on their numerical superiority. Early on, it enabled them to achieve success. But that didn't last long. The Germans soon brought in reinforcements, including tanks, planes, and artillery that were no match for the ill-supplied Poles.

Halina's brother, Zygmund, was in the north of Warsaw, which the Germans subdued quickly. Halina was in another part of the city, where the Home Army was stronger and could sustain the fight longer. The demands of war had prevented her from seeing her brother for quite some time. She missed him terribly, but knowing Zygmund as she did, she knew he was doing everything he could to help the war effort. Eventually, word reached her that Zygmund had been in the street during a bombing. As he was running for cover, he spotted a badly wounded Polish man lying in the debris. Unwilling to leave him there to die, Zygmund picked the man up and managed to carry him all the way to a hospital.

Then he ran to his mother's flat to warn her the Gestapo was on its way. "Mother, you must leave quickly! The Gestapo is coming, and we may be picked up. Hurry! They will be here in less than an hour!"

But Mrs. Peszke could not go anywhere. Her older sister and brother-in-law were in her home because her brother-in-law had just been hit on the head by bricks from a building that had been bombed, and Mrs. Peszke was tending to the wound. As Zygmund predicted, the Germans swarmed into the building within the hour, rounding up everyone who appeared strong enough to be shipped off to labor camps.

However, they left Halina's mother, sister, and brother-in-law alone, probably because of their age and their poor health. But Zygmund, who had run back down to the street, was arrested and shipped off to Auschwitz. It would be a long time before Halina and her mother would learn what happened to him.

సా

The battle that Gen. Tadeusz Bór-Komorowski said would last only two days dragged on for more than two grueling months—from August 1 to October 2. Before it was over, the extent of the atrocities against the Polish fighters and innocent civilians astonished everyone. An order issued by Hitler's right-hand man, Heinrich Himmler, was intended to send a message to all Europeans under Nazi control. The order was to kill all of Warsaw's residents, take no prisoners, and level the city.

What started as an organized battle plan evolved into a vicious, monumental street fight—block by block, building by building. Many years later, Halina described what it was like to move through the fog of the war:

A day or two before the insurrection started, we already knew that it was about to begin and only awaited orders from General Komorowski. The young people were in their underground shelters, ready with a meager supply of small arms. [Of the estimated 40,000 fighters, only 2,500 had weapons.]

For weeks women had been gathering food to provide for the people who were ready to take the fight to the Germans. It was interesting to see these women storing enough food, not for the two-day engagement they were told it would be, but for at least a month.

When I looked at the "army" of combatants gathered in the cellars waiting the order to commence, I saw young faces, boys and girls really, which made me wonder how prepared we were to go up in battle against hardened professional soldiers.

While I was packing my rucksack with a change of clothing, soap, toiletries, a cup, all of the bandages and medical supplies I had gathered, I did a very foolish thing. I left my precious Bible behind. My thinking at the time was that when the fighting begins, I will be fighting and running and hiding from the enemy; so it's very unlikely I will have time for reading. And if we are victorious, there will be many places where I can find Bibles. The best outcome will allow me to come back home and retrieve my Bible and books.

Time would tell just how wrong I was to think like this. It would be a long wait before I ever again held a Bible. And after my capture and internment as a prisoner of war, the one possession that I needed desperately to sustain hope and comfort was my Bible. It was a hard, actually bitter, lesson that *affected my conduct for the rest of my life. Whatever else was left behind, I would never again be apart from the Word of God.*

At the outset of the fighting, the Polish Resistance pushed the Germans out of many areas of the city and recaptured the gas, electric, and water plants, enabling hospitals to resume services with power restored. Armament and printing facilities also were recaptured, allowing communication to resume through newspapers the occupiers had shut down.

A highpoint of the insurrection came when the Poles took the large Wehrmacht warehouse in the Wola district where the Germans stored food, military supplies, and uniforms. The Resistance fighters promptly dressed in some of the uniforms, leaving only the red and white armbands of the Polish Home Army visible. The ruse allowed fighters to pass some German outposts without being detected.

But the Germans began sending in more troops, tanks, and heavy weapons. Moving about in the open then became treacherous:

We decided that there was a way to get around in the city without showing our faces. As most of the houses were connected, it was possible to break through cellar basement walls and open doors to move from one place to another undetected. This saved a lot of lives because the enemy had begun placing tanks at the end of streets where their guns could reach anyone who happened to be caught in the open. When we were blocked by sewers or other obstacles, we worked side by side to make barricades from paving blocks.

The fighting during the day was terrible because the

enemy had tanks placed at the end of every major street. These barricades were put up during the night when the tanks were not shelling us. During the day, the shooting was almost constant, which made crossing, even with the barricades, very dangerous. On one occasion I was crossing a street, the Alley of Jerusalem, which ran through the whole of Warsaw. I was with a number of others. As we moved across, the tank at the end of the street began shooting, and a shell exploded nearly in our faces. Miraculously, I was not hit; but the woman immediately in front of me was killed.

While we were paying the price in blood to make gains, there was, especially in the first days, a feeling of near euphoria when we would see lines of German prisoners walking with hands raised in surrender to our men. Courtyards were used as dressing stations where our girl nurses worked to bandage and aid the wounded. It didn't matter whether victims wore a German uniform or were one of our own. Everyone was treated with the same respect and level of care. We were careful to do everything according to the Geneva Convention, even though the same courtesy was not given to us. We were treated as renegades. If we were caught or wounded, we would be killed immediately.

When the tide turned and the Nazis gained the upper hand, the slaughter was unrelenting. In the Wola district, where the Germans had been humiliated, they held mass executions of Polish fighters and civilians. When the massacre ended, 40,000 Polish people had been systematically killed. Germany intended to let the Poles know they would break their will to resist and force them to surrender. Yet the result was the opposite. For Halina and everyone who participated in the uprising, surrender meant death. To die fighting was preferable to being executed.

Some in the Resistance, however, could not keep going. Their wounds crippled them, forcing their compatriots to leave them behind. In the case of civilians, many had nowhere to hide. Their fates were sealed. In one district, the Nazis used Polish women as human shields while attacking insurgent positions.

In the Wola and St. Lazarus hospitals, the Germans murdered 1,360 patients and staff. In some of the field hospitals, they burned the wounded alive in their beds. Mass executions took place in districts occupied by the Wehrmacht; and death squads moved from house to house, killing everyone inside.

In a strange way, the worst of times sometimes create inexplicable contradictions. For the people of Poland, the war aroused their love of country and triumphantly displayed their determination to survive against all odds. For the Jewish people, whose excruciating suffering the world will never fully realize, the war increased their love for their homeland in the Middle East, which had been under foreign occupation for 2,000 years.

For Halina, it led to a love story that united her in marriage in 1944 to a man she fought beside as a soldier at the barricades, on the streets, and through the tunnels. Samuel had become the love of her life. Despite the war, they dared to dream of a life together, unaware they would soon be separated and not know when, where, or if they would see each other again.

In late September 1944, American planes delivered a huge airdrop of food and supplies. Insurgents were able to retrieve about 16 tons, a mere 20 percent of the cargo. The rest was captured by the Germans. Although the airdrop briefly lifted Polish spirits, it was too little too late. The Polish fighters were falling to superior firepower and larger numbers of troops. Halina and her friends were not willing to give up. But by the end of September, it became clear their time was running out.

CHAPTER 6

The Final March

Warsaw was symbolic. It was Hitler's last-gasp attempt to exhibit the imperial power of the Third Reich. Polish soldiers were using the sewers to escape into the center of the city where things were still relatively secure. The sewers, however, filled with vermin, stench, and slime, were a trial in themselves. Some who survived the Wehrmacht guns could not survive the sewers. Even for the healthier soldiers, the putrid conditions and close quarters slowed their progress, as did carrying their wounded comrades whom they refused to abandon to the enemy unless absolutely necessary.

Halina and the others assigned as nurses waited to receive the people who were lifted to the street, washing their grimy faces and tending to their wounds. "These men are heroes," she told another worker. "Their will to survive and to help their fellow soldiers, even to the point that they are willing to die for one another, shows their love for each other and the country."

Despite all their sacrifices, it soon became obvious the insurgents would lose. Halina knew the consequences for the Polish fighters would be especially grave because the Germans did not consider them prisoners of war. That meant the Nazis would immediately kill them or send them to concentration camps as "dangerous elements." As a lieutenant in the Home Army, Halina knew she would be executed.

Then something happened that altered the outcome. After delaying their decision considerably, Britain and the

United States granted official Allied combatant status to the Polish Home Army. They did so hoping Polish prisoners would be treated as regular combat troops and be held as prisoners of war (POWs), rather than as radical insurgents to be summarily killed.

When representatives of General Bór-Komorowski met with German General Erich von dem Bach to surrender, the Germans agreed to guarantee full Geneva Convention treatment to the insurgents. The decision not only helped the Poles, but it also benefited the thousands of young Germans who were now in jeopardy of being captured by the Allies who each day were moving closer to Germany. Applying the rules of the Geneva Convention would secure their treatment as POWs.

When the Polish soldiers gathered to lay down their arms and prepare to begin life as prisoners of war, the Germans were surprised to see how few arms there were to collect. In the last days of the insurrection, the Poles often stood in the streets and moved about with weapons but no ammunition, giving the appearance of being ready to resist but having no real means of doing so. Silently, Halina and her comrades passed by large boxes and deposited their meager firearms. Then she and the remainder of the force, an estimated 15,000 people, gathered in the city and lined up in rows of eight, as commanded:

We began the march in complete silence. It was as if we were covered by a blanket of sadness. As we marched through the streets of the city, almost every street where great houses had stood was piled with rubble. Some walls were still standing, and here and there the remains of houses still stood. But through the empty windows we could see only burned-out rooms. The German incendiary bombs had been mercilessly effective in burning any building they hit.

We walked kilometer after kilometer through a dead city. Not one person was seen. One of two things had happened: either the owners had been killed in the bombings, or they had been driven out of the city days before. Outside Warsaw, we saw Polish peasants lining the sides of the roads. They were mostly poor people from the villages we were passing by. Some of them had prepared small loaves of bread that they began throwing to us as we walked by. For us, the future was an open question. Only our enemies knew where we were going. All of the stories we had heard and atrocities we had seen were passing through our heads. One thing we knew, our beloved Warsaw would never stand again as we had known it. It was as though we had just passed through a huge cemetery.

Hitler's forces had leveled Warsaw. It was a wasteland of debris and smoldering ruins. After the Polish soldiers were force-marched out of the city, massive looting began. Delegations from German municipalities rushed in to take anything that had not already been confiscated by the Wehrmacht. After the collapse of the Resistance, the Nazis plundered the city, filling thousands of railway cars with furniture, personal belongings, and factory equipment and carried it all away. Following the looting, blocks of abandoned structures were burned; and monuments honoring Polish notables, as well as municipal buildings, were blown up.

What happened to Warsaw surpassed what happens to most cities engaged in a losing battle. It was ripped open and ravished, the victim of the scorched-earth policy that emanated from Hitler's demented mind. Near the end of the war, Hitler ranted that he had been lied to by his own people, claimed that the Germans had not fought with enough heroism, and declared that they "deserve to perish." And with that crazed appraisal, he refused to surrender and allowed Berlin to be destroyed.

⁖

Halina was now officially a POW. For the moment, her mission was to stay on her feet and endure the seemingly endless march to wherever the Germans were taking her. The bread the peasants had cast their way did much more for the Polish prisoners than express the peasants' love for them. Every loaf caught was broken into small pieces and distributed like manna from heaven:

> *I do remember when I got such a piece. It was a bit of soft roll, and I put it in my mouth and munched it slowly. And I remember keeping it in my mouth for a long time. It was in the strength of this little piece that I could walk. It was amazing how, by God's grace, these little pieces allowed me the strength to walk probably 18 kilometers [11 miles] more before we stopped for the night.*
>
> *We finally reached Ozarów, a place west of Warsaw. After standing for a long time, we were ushered into a huge building that was part of a factory. Once inside, there was not enough room to stretch out— only enough room to sit arm to arm. Some of us talked about how easy it would be to escape from this place and run away. But that was of no interest to me. Not only did I not have the strength, but I wanted to be as far west as possible (I hoped in Germany) when the Allies would come to liberate us. The best prospect was that, if we were freed by*

the Allies, I could return to Poland and put my life back together.

Early the next morning, the Polish soldiers were roused from their sleep and lined up to march to a place where there were long lines of railroad cars ordinarily used to carry cattle. With so many prisoners, loading them into the cars took several hours. Halina and the women were locked into a tightly packed space with no ventilation or anything resembling a toilet.

Suddenly, one of the young women called out, "I can fix that," holding up a small penknife.

"How will you do anything with such a small knife?" another asked in an almost mocking tone.

"Just wait and see," said the girl. She squatted on the floor and began to whittle away at the wood. It was slow work, but she was persistent; and before long she cried out triumphantly, "I've cut through! Come take a look. When I've made it a little bigger, we'll have a toilet and a window down to the tracks that will let in some fresh air."

The train lumbered along slowly for several hours before it pulled onto a sidetrack and stopped near a small town. When the doors were thrown open, blinding light and fresh air flooded in. The women were overcome with relief. An added blessing was that they finally were able to get out and stretch their stiff legs. Although Halina could not identify the location, she knew they were still in Poland:

As I looked toward the town, I saw people coming toward us carrying large urns of hot coffee and piles of bread. A man from the group told us that they belonged to an organization that was called "The Main Council of Care." Their leaders had made an agreement with the Germans to be allowed to bring bread and drink to the prisoners when the trains were stopped near the town. To eat and drink was wonderful, and what made the experience even better was that we again looked on some pleasant Polish faces.

Their turning up when they did was for me like a miracle—our beloved Lord providing for us when there was no help from our captors. I did think again of what the Bible says about being careful to entertain strangers because we might be ministering to angels without knowing it. Only this time it would be the "angels" ministering to us.

However we looked at it, their intervention with bread and drink would be all that we would get for the three days it took to arrive at our destination.

After three days, the trains came to a halt, the doors were opened, and the prisoners were ordered off. Halina knew she was now in Germany, but she did not know where. "Perhaps," she thought, "it is a concentration camp."

After the men and women were separated, we were told to march. Soon we began passing camps where there were scores of Polish people. Some of them were from Warsaw—civilians who were allowed to leave and then were picked up and taken to this camp.

As we passed, we didn't dare to talk to them. We just had to keep marching on, smiling to each other. When we were ordered to stop, I saw the barbed wire and the gates into two camps side by side. We were marched into one, while the men were marched into the other. Between the two camps was a space large enough for German soldiers to walk with their guns, keeping watch that no one would attempt to escape.

After we were lined up and counted—something that would be done twice a day—we were divided into groups of 40 and led into the barracks. My bed was made of wood slats with a thin layer of hay serving as a mattress. Each of us was issued a thin, worn-out blanket that was no match for the bitterly cold winters we would be subjected to.

But there was food. Each of us was given a dish of potatoes—five or six small ones—cooked by Russian prisoners who worked in the kitchen. In Poland potatoes were something we always took for granted. They were always there on the table in one form or another. But seeing the little morsels that would bring a measure of strength back to my exhausted body looked like life itself. Actually, I had not seen a potato since the Warsaw uprising. Now, on the plate before me, they became a feast. We sat together and slowly savored our potatoes, skins and all.

Then it was off to be counted again before we were allowed to sleep. For that first night behind the wire, the hard slats on my bunk were of no consequence. Nothing mattered but the chance to sleep. Tomorrow would have to take care of itself. I was alive, and for me the war was over. That was enough.

ॐ

Life in the barracks was an endless round of boredom broken by hours of standing in lines to be counted. The German commandants at the camps were paranoid about possible escapes. For Halina and her fellow prisoners, the counting seemed a useless exercise. No one was of a mind to scale the barbed wire and run for it. They were confident the Allies were coming, and they wanted to be there to greet them on liberation day.

"We've been talking about it, and we would like for you to do something for us," a prisoner told Halina one day.

"Of course. You know I'll do anything I can to help any of you. What is it you want me to do?"

"We know you can speak English. And we expect that very soon the Americans and British will come to free us. We would like to learn enough English to speak with them when they arrive."

So the young lieutenant became the camp English professor, a roll she relished so much that hour-long sessions often stretched into two hours or more. Unfortunately, the lessons were cut short by the return of an old physical adversary. Halina began to feel ill and suffered frequent sensations of weakness until, during one English lesson, she passed out. The women carried her back to her bed. Lack of proper nourishment, along with severe winter conditions, exacerbated her already weakened condition, affecting her balance for months. Her poor health made life more difficult because the Germans were moving prisoners from one camp to another as the Allies advanced. Before the war ended, Halina and her friends were moved five times.

When she and several hundred women from the Polish Home Army arrived at the prisoner of war camp in Altenburg, Germany, they had a brief respite from their usual, depressing surroundings. Instead of line after line of barracks, with not even a blade of grass in sight, they were able to see the town on a hill above them. The installation where they were being kept was in a low-lying area that provided a view of picturesque Altenburg, with its majestic castle and quaint shops.

Seeing people milling about on the streets was like having an open window on a magnificent portrait of normal life. Even though they could not go anywhere, the women were encouraged by the psychological effect of viewing an existence that seemed much like what they had known before the war. They savored what they saw as they lay on their slatted bunks with thin straw fillings in the frigid night.

Each day when the prisoners gathered to get their daily rations, they were handed a piece of black bread and a cup of sugarless herb tea. Once every 24 hours they were given bowls of thin soup that perhaps had a single carrot as the main attraction. On that meager fare they were expected to survive.

A pleasant feature of Altenburg was the presence of a prisoner from the Netherlands who for some reason was treated better than the Poles. The man was drawn to Halina because she could speak English, making it possible for them to spend a few minutes talking together. He was sympathetic to her physical condition and insisted she share his portion of black bread, which was always larger than what the Germans doled out to the Poles. If wood was available, he gathered it, filled the small stove in the barracks, and lit a fire. Though it did not provide enough heat for comfort, the fire took a slight edge off the winter cold that invaded their quarters.

In spite of the harsh conditions and the long hours standing to be counted or lectured, there was a creative inventiveness among the inmates. The prisoners formed classes and took turns educating one another on a variety of subjects. Although there wasn't a blade of grass to be found, one woman taught a class in gardening—a skill the women hoped to apply to actual soil when the war was over.

Some of the prisoners were historians. They met together and conceived a plan to teach aspects of Polish history. The lessons complemented the English Halina had taught, as well as other courses offered by others who were experienced in their fields.

A favorite attraction was the performances of two lovely Polish actresses who were prisoners. Educated in the works of Poland's great poets, the women profoundly touched the other inmates with patriotic poems impeccably recited. It seemed their repertoire was endless, and their listeners did not want them to stop. Though the group was diverse, every woman in it had been deprived of what she loved and held dear, and these moving performances kindled an extraordinary depth of feeling within them all.

⁓

It was no secret Halina was a believer in Jesus. So it seemed natural for some of the older women to ask her to lead the group in prayer. There was a special urgency to pray when they received word they were scheduled to move to another camp. They were concerned about where they were going. Would they be separated, never to see one another again? Would they be moved from prisoner-of-war camps into prisons or concentration camps? Such things had happened before when younger prisoners were removed from the group and hauled off to work camps. So Halina prayed:

> *In the barracks we would stand in a circle, take hands, and pray. Our prayers began with praying for one another, and we would commit all of our soldiers to God's keeping and grace. We remembered*

also to pray for our dear country and the leaders in the government in exile.

We also prayed for the German people because we believed that most of them wished for peace the same as we did. Our prayers continued for an end to the war and for those who were fighting to liberate us.

The prayer circle became so much a part of our day that the girls asked me if we could have prayer in the evenings as well. So I arranged for us to join in prayer after we were in our bunks and ready to sleep. It was a great source of comfort to us all. There were only three or four atheists in the entire group who refused to take part in the prayer times. But we did pray for them too.

These prayer sessions opened many opportunities for the women to open up and come to me with questions about spiritual things. Some were angry and confused. Others had never come to grips with their spiritual needs and wanted help on what they should do. It was during these talks that I fully realized how great a mistake I had made when I was packing my rucksack and left out my precious Bible. Now I knew that it was the only thing that I needed most. I could help these girls by telling them what the Bible said about their situations, but I was not able to open the Book and read to them. Neither could I enjoy for myself the comfort and joy that comes from quiet times together with the Lord and His Word.

Perhaps in the back of my mind I felt that there would never be a problem in picking up a Bible somewhere. It had never been a problem to do so *before. As a matter of fact, I was surrounded by Bibles as long as I could remember. But now no one around me had a copy that I could borrow for my own comfort or use in working with women in need of spiritual counsel.*

Halina's group was moved to another camp. For the most part, the prisoners there were French and English, and the camp's commandant was reasonable:

When our captain went to him and requested a minister to come and hold services for our women, he agreed and sent for a priest. When the man came, he held the service in French because many of the one thousand officers incarcerated there understood French.

After the sermon, he asked how many would like to participate in communion. It may have surprised him to see nearly a full thousand women line up to take communion. It took a long time to complete the service, but the women, virtually all of whom were Catholic, felt a great sense of joy.

The German commandant was made aware of Halina's inability to walk at times and ordered her into the hospital for treatment, where she received excellent care and rested in a comfortable, normal bed. When the food service came by, she received the same fare as the wounded German soldiers—a large bowl of soup that was nothing short of what she had dreamed of in her bouts of sickness. It had meat, plenty of vegetables, bread, and other nourishing ingredients. After eight days, she regained her strength and was walking again.

Almost as good as the treatment and food was her position near a window where she could look outside. The first thing she saw in the distance was a tree with green leaves filling its branches. The welcome sight caused her to think of all the good things life had brought her way before the war.

"I have what may seem a strange request to you," Halina told the friendly young nurse attending her.

"And what request would that be?" responded her attendant.

"Would it be too much for me to ask that you bring me a leaf from that tree?"

"I don't know why not. I pass by it every morning on my way to the hospital."

The next morning, the nurse delivered on her promise; and the green leaf, with all its symbolic treasure, floated in a glass of water by Halina's bed.

Her rejuvenation was short-lived, however, because after she returned to the camp, her condition again deteriorated. She was sent back to the hospital, but this one was filled mostly with Italian patients. Once allies, Germany and Italy were no longer friendly. Hitler had broken ties with Italian dictator Benito Mussolini, captured many Italians, and turned former friends into prisoners of war. Yet the Italians were well-treated and friendly. And one in particular was a great help to Halina:

One day, during a conversation with an Italian patient, we were talking about spiritual things. When I told him about my big mistake in leaving my Bible behind, he said, "That is not a problem. I can get you a Bible."

The next day he was back at my bedside with a small New Testament in his hand. "Here it is," he said. "Now it will never be far from you."

I couldn't thank him enough. It was like I was receiving life again. Oh, what a joy it was. I would read it and read it without stopping. I could now translate to fellow prisoners who were also sick and confined to their bunks. What a joy it was. I was so happy—so, so happy.

CHAPTER 7

Say Hello to Freedom

The last stop for Halina in the prisons of the Third Reich was a camp outside Erfurt, Germany. In the early 1500s, Erfurt was the home of the venerated priest turned reformer, Martin Luther, who is extolled as the father of Protestantism. Luther's later, vehement anti-Semitism seemed to set the tone for Hitler's legacy of hatred toward the Jews. Luther's eight-point plan to rid Germany of the Jewish people sums up the depth of his hostility: "If we wash our hands of the Jews' blasphemy and not share in their guilt, we have to part company with them. They must be driven from our country. . . . We must drive them out like mad dogs."

For the most part, the fortunes of Germany's 600,000 Jewish people rose and fell with the country's economic good times and bad times. But even when times were good, anti-Semitism was never far away. In the 19th century, German philosophers, university professors, and some prominent authors were already concocting the brew that would distill into the "final solution." German author-philosopher Paul de Lagarde wrote, "I have long been convinced that Jewry constitutes the cancer in all our life; as Jews, they are strangers in any European state and as such they are nothing but spreaders of decay."[1]

Near Erfurt was the city of Weimar, the pre-Hitler seat of governmental authority. Between 1919 and 1933, the German government was referred to as the "Weimar Republic." Weimar was a democratic republic governed by a constitution written in the city of Weimar. Historians have held that, on paper, the Weimar Constitution was a brilliant document; and Germany under the Weimar Republic was a true democracy.

However, the government in the 1920s had huge problems that stemmed from the country's defeat in World War I. High unemployment (6 million without jobs), serious financial problems, and rampant inflation provided fertile soil for Hitler and the fledgling Nazi movement to sow their seeds of hatred and blame the Jewish people for Germany's woes. The Nazis held huge rallies in Weimar and, with pageantry and promises, won the loyalty of an aggrieved and deprived populace.

By 1933 the Nazis were voted in as the solution to Germany's woes. What the optimistic Germans received for their political investment was the destruction of the constitution; the end of representative government; and the installation of a violent dictatorship led by a ruthless, bloodthirsty psychopath who would bring ruin to his people.

Ironically, the city that celebrated throwing away its future by believing one man with charisma and promises is the same city that saw the notorious Buchenwald concentration camp go up nearby, a mere four years after Hitler ascended to power. Among the first internees were approximately 10,000 Jewish people, brought there as political prisoners after the "Night of Broken Glass" (Kristallnacht) in 1938 when they were viciously attacked.

When they arrived, the Jewish prisoners were subjected to extraordinarily cruel treatment. They were worked between 14 and 15 hours a day, generally in the infamous Buchenwald quarry. Besides being forced into abominable living conditions, they were used for diabolical medical experiments. Buchenwald was a notorious facility.

When the war began, prisoners from at least 30 countries

were forced through its gates. In addition to the main facility, the Buchenwald system included some 130 satellite camps. Molsdorf was one of Buchenwald's small satellite camps located near Erfurt. It consisted of seven rickety barracks built in a swampy area and capable of containing about 400 prisoners. And Molsdorf is where Halina and her friends were taken.

Conditions were extremely difficult. There were no stoves for heat, despite winter nights that were bitterly cold. There were no provisions for cooking, and gathering firewood for any purpose was strictly forbidden. Hygienic conditions were poor, and more than 100 prisoners a day commonly reported sick. To make matters more depressing, the women were forbidden to express their religious faith or conduct religious services.

Being near Buchenwald brought an even greater weight of sadness to Halina, one she would carry the rest of her life. She learned what happened to her beloved brother, Zygmund. While in Auschwitz, he had met a doctor friend he had known and began helping him care for the sick, who were placed in separate barracks. No medicine was available, so all that could be done was to take their temperatures and make them as comfortable as possible.

Then one day a truck came filled with Ukrainian prisoners. Looking into the makeshift infirmary, the Germans saw Zygmund standing there alone and ordered him into the vehicle. With a full cargo of prisoners, the truck rolled toward Germany and its destination: Buchenwald. Approximately three weeks later, Zygmund was dead. He was brutally beaten to death. Zygmund's murder weighed heavily on Halina. He was the brother she had loved and admired all her life. With him gone, the world seemed a very different place.

Murder was common in Buchenwald. Chilling reports circulated about inmates being killed, some in grotesque ways. Halina was told, for example, how SS guards would push a prisoner's head into an overflowing toilet until the person drowned. It was not uncommon for inmates to go insane because of beatings, grueling work, and lack of food. Like Zygmund, hundreds died within a few weeks of their arrival.

Any one of these elements could easily have broken Halina's spirits and that of the other Polish women. Yet they opted to continue, as much as possible, their activities in education, theater, and reading that they had instituted in previous camps. Soldiers in every sense of the word, they shared a steadfast determination to survive with dignity regardless of their situation.

When Halina arrived at Molsdorf, she had not eaten properly in weeks. The Allies were pounding Germany with bombs, and their rapid advances made food hard to come by, especially for prisoners. Exhausted from the journey to the camp, Halina lay in her bunk doubled over in pain and weeping softly. Her stomach hurt so badly it had become unbearable. Almost unconsciously, she prayed the Lord's prayer:

> Our Father which art in heaven, hallowed be thy name. Thy kingdom come. Thy will be done in earth, as it is heaven. Give us this day our daily bread. And forgive us our debts, as we forgive our debtors. And lead us not into temptation, but deliver us from evil: for thine is the kingdom, and the power, and the glory, for ever. Amen (Mt. 6:9–13).

When she came to the words "give us this day our daily bread," she found herself pleading that God would supply her with something to eat. Then suddenly, the pain was gone. Doctors say that in extreme cases of food deprivation, a person's intestines shrink so much they no longer feel hunger pains. Halina's explanation is somewhat different:

> *I know that a moment before, I had been in pain, with tears running down my face and asking the Lord to feed me. And He did! It was not with physical food, as I was asking, but by just stopping my pain. It was bread from heaven. Not the kind I was seeking, but really more satisfying. From that day until I was liberated, I never felt such pain in my stomach again.*

By 1945 Halina had endured nearly six years of war—years that had turned a bright 20-year-old who relished every new experience into a battle-hardened young woman on the verge of mental and physical exhaustion. Yet conditions were so terrible that sleeping was difficult:

> *Once we were down in our beds, visitors would arrive. They were rats—lots and lots of rats—big ones, accompanied by hordes of mice and hungry bedbugs that would drop down on us from holes in the ceiling. We would wrap up tightly in our blankets to try and keep covered. We were often wakened by our visitors running across our bodies on their way to the shelves holding our belongings, searching for whatever morsels they might find. The best way to keep anything edible was to put it under the straw mattress and, as much as one could, keep a hand on it.*

> *One elderly lady was a scientist specializing in biology and nature studies. Her love for nature was a bit, to my mind, bizarre. She began talking to the rats as if they were people. While we were frightened, she was passing part of her night conversing with rodents.*

Halina needed relief and comfort. And in those miserable circumstances, there existed only one source from which it could come:

I was lying on my bunk, and it was about noon. My eyes were fixed on the ceiling. Suddenly, before my eyes (I was certainly awake and not asleep) I saw a beautiful, blue heaven. I thought it was like one a person would see in a place like Italy. Not a cloud in the sky, but just endless blue. And then I saw an opening very, very high above me. Above this opening, there were hundreds or more of little beings whom I thought must be angels or people in heaven, in long white robes bathed in sunshine. I didn't see any wings, but I was sure they were people or, most likely, angels floating above me.

And I knew the Lord Jesus Christ was farther behind. I didn't see Him, but I knew He was there and that God Himself who keeps the universe in His hands was also somehow there. It was not what I saw that was so comforting, but from this opening in heaven came a wonderful feeling of perfect happiness in my inner being, into my soul. I was filled with joy, heavenly joy. I was consciously praising God in my spirit, loving Him, rejoicing that there is such a place as heaven. I was longing that in good time, God's time, I will be there, because of the sacrifice made for me by the Lord Jesus Christ.

I was glad for those who went before us, my dear ones, who were in such happiness. I could never begin to imagine such happiness as I was feeling. I felt this spirit of happiness coming from the opening in heaven, right into my being.

As if to assure me that this was not just a dream, a

> *few days later it happened again. To me, that was a confirmation. It was always at noon when I was not asleep. Some, who were not there, may disagree. But to me, there on my bunk in that awful place, it was very real.*

Unknown to the women prisoners, the Red Cross had been searching for them for months. Their efforts were fruitless, partly because the prisoners were being rapidly moved from one place to another. Finally the Red Cross learned that they were being held at Molsdorf and began sending packages to them.

After long months of deprivation, the women could not restrain their joy when they opened the little parcels. Inside they found dried bread, chocolate, sugar, and some tins of canned food. The delivery temporarily made them feel like they had all been invited to a party with the Red Cross as their host.

As Halina slowly ate food from the parcel, she began thinking of another time when a friend in the women's camp held out a hand in kindness. On rare occasions, a parcel for the woman made it through the red tape and pilferage and arrived at the camp. Inside the woman found, among other things, two eggs still relatively fresh—raw, but edible.

"Here," she said to Halina, holding one out to her. "You take it. We'll be moving again soon, and you will need your strength."

"Oh, no, I cannot take food out of your mouth. It was intended for you. Eat them," Halina told her.

"Halina, I will not take no for an answer. Come, sit here by me, and we will eat together."

Knowing further protests would be futile, Halina

reluctantly sat down with the kind woman who, with a smile, held out an egg and a small piece of bread. Together they ate the precious food. The gift was small, but the act of kindness established something much larger. Even though they hardly saw each other again, a bond was forged, as well as a memory Halina would cherish the rest of her life:

These moments brought wonderful things into our lives. Yes, we were in a war from which many would never return. But so many were totally unselfish and were always ready to share whatever they received and was precious to them, however small, with those around them. There was a genuine love for our camp neighbors. It was the kind of love patterned after the words of the Lord Jesus Christ, when He said, "Thou shalt love thy neighbor as thyself" [Mt. 19:19]. And also after Leviticus 19: "The stranger that dwelleth with you shall be unto you as one born among you, and thou shalt love him as thyself; for ye were strangers in the land of Egypt: I am the Lord your God" [v. 34].

It is the kind of love that cannot be explained to those who have never gone through extreme hardships together. Somehow, my life was changed— something I would carry with me forever.

Eventually, the prisoners began to hear the crescendo of gunfire that seemed to be coming closer by the hour. The fighting went on for days:

We now began to feel that the war would soon come to an end. And I was sure of it when the order came that everyone able to walk in our barracks was to prepare for a quick exit out of the camp. We were to be moved to a camp inside the center of Germany. There were about 40 of us who were not fit enough for another march, so we were to be left behind.

I was hopeful that my feelings that the war was near an end were correct, but I was sad to see my friends—people who had been my officers in the army, and all of the rest who had passed so many trials together—preparing to march. All that was left now was to say goodbye and wonder what would happen to them, and to me, for that matter.

What was left for us were a few guards and the German women who cooked for us, never much, a watery bowl of soup, a bit of bread, and perhaps a small carrot. One of our guards was an elderly man, obviously too old to be on the front line. From time to time he would come to the barbed wire, call one of us over, and produce an onion for us to share. He did it all the while we were still in the camp. One onion, kindly given.

I often wondered if the man was a believer. I suspect he was, for one reason: If he had been caught passing an onion through the fence, he would have been severely punished. Perhaps even shot. The Germans were living in a near-starvation situation themselves, and there was little sympathy for those who consorted, even in the smallest way, with prisoners. And so it was when the end was near.

৵

On April 11, 1945, the tanks of U.S. Gen. George Patton's Third Army rolled up to the enclosures surrounding Buchenwald. What transpired over the next few days reflected what was taking place in the satellite camps, such as the one where Halina and her friends were held.

Patton's tanks first rolled through the barbed-wire fence at the back of the main camp. "The roar of the tanks made us shiver from happiness," recalled one prisoner.

A young man named Shiku Smilovic, in the children's block at Buchenwald, later explained what it was like to be set free:

> Everybody was running towards the American liberators, hugging and kissing them; they were practically tearing them apart. Everybody wanted to touch them and embrace them. Tears were running freely from everyone, including the big strong black Americans. People were dancing and screaming: "We are free! We are free!" American planes were overhead dropping balloons with the American flag attached to them. The skies were full of parachutes with food supplies dropping all over the place. What a sight! People were going wild tearing the supplies apart and having a feast. Singing and crying at the same time, without realizing that their stomachs were not used to that much food.[2]

Among the prisoners liberated was a young Elie (Eliezer) Wiesel, later to become a famous novelist, journalist, and Nobel Peace Prize winner. Wiesel was 17 when the Americans arrived at Buchenwald. In March 1944, the Germans had occupied his hometown of Sighet, Romania, in the Carpathian Mountains, and prepared to deport the Jews to prison camps. Although the Wiesels' Christian maid urged them to hide in her mountain hut, they stayed with the Jewish community. Eventually, they were loaded into cattle cars with 80 others and deported. Weisel would later say, "Life in the cattle cars was the death of my adolescence."

Elie and his father were transferred from another camp to Buchenwald, where his father died of dysentery, starvation, and exhaustion. Young Elie was sent to join 600 other children in a cellblock. On April 6, 1945, guards told Elie and the others they would no longer be fed. The Germans began evacuating the camp, killing 10,000 prisoners a day. In the early evening of April 11, Elie stood in a group, watching the American troops enter the enclosure to liberate Buchenwald.

U.S. Gen. Dwight David Eisenhower, supreme commander of the Allied Forces in Europe, arrived with his staff on April 14 to inspect the camp. They were shown great mounds of human bodies, piled like lumber 10 feet high.

They just stood there and stared in amazement. Eisenhower and his aides removed their helmets and stood silent for some time out of respect for the dead. Then the general turned to his staff. "Who would do such a thing to human beings?" he asked. "I can't believe what I see."

Eisenhower ordered the entire city of Weimar—all men, women, and children—brought in to see the sight. Then he hurriedly walked away. "I had enough," he said. "I think I've seen enough today."

As he toured the camps, he told his people, "Get it all on record now—get the films, get the witnesses—because somewhere down the road of history some b_____ will get up and say that this never happened."

Later, Gen. Eisenhower uttered what would become the consummate observation: "[If] the American soldiers did not know what they were fighting for until they saw the concentration camps, then they at least knew what they were fighting against."

As the first group of emaciated prisoners slowly made their way out of the barracks toward the Americans, they looked like walking corpses—bones draped in rags. But they had survived.

Dining at the Castle

The Germans had moved most of the women at the beginning of April 1945. Those who remained, including Halina, were in the infirmary. The Americans were surprised to find them lying on the floor, side by side. When questioned, they explained they were military POWs from Warsaw. The Americans then told them they were free:

We were told that we were free to leave the camp if we wished. However, at that time we were afraid to leave, and stayed there until things were more settled.

We also asked the German guard who had been so kind to us if he would stay and continue to act as our guard, which he did. But maybe it was not the best thing for him to do. Some days later when the Americans returned to the camp, we were asked about the soldier. They told him to get in their jeep as a prisoner.

I asked them to leave him alone, because he was a good German. The man replied, "There are no good Germans," and they sped away. I was deeply ashamed that I didn't do more to protect this man who had done so much for us. The Americans were looking for Gestapo and were in no mood to stay in one place for long, fearing snipers or other Nazis still on the loose in the area.

So, all we could do was pray that our friend would be treated kindly as a prisoner and could return safely to his family after the war.

A few days later a soldier arrived at the camp and asked if anyone could speak English. I told him that

I could answer for the group and informed him that we were all officers of the Polish army. After our talk, he invited a companion and me to join the American officers for dinner. To my surprise, we were taken to a grand castle where we were greeted by officers, many of whom were graduates of West Point.

For a few hours, it was like I had entered another world. To be treated with respect and kindness was something I hadn't experienced in such surroundings for all the years of the war. Now I was eating a delicious meal, with no feeling of fear or threat of being beaten or badly abused.

Soon after, all 40 of us were taken to a lovely part of the Erfurt German hospital where we were well treated and made comfortable. But our stay was not to be long. The Americans and Russians, who were at the time allies, had an agreement that Erfurt would be occupied by Russia.

Ironically, we were on the move again. But there was a big difference. This time we were not in boxcars with no windows, heat, or room to lie down. I could look out the windows of the train and see the countryside of one of the most beautiful areas of Germany.

Although I was still very ill, and without knowledge of what was wrong or why I did not continue to improve, there was much to be happy about. Husbands of some of the girls were beginning to arrive; and the sight of the reunions encouraged us all, giving hope that it would soon be the same for us. The only stain was to see a young soldier who came looking for his wife and we had to tell him that he was too late. She had taken ill when we were still in the camp with no doctors or proper medical care.

But now, after all of the suffering and hardships, we could see the future in the eyes of those found by their loved ones. And, I think, that most were ready to leave the lives we had known as soldiers behind us.

[1] Cited in "Germany and anti-Semitism: the 19th century," The Danish Center for Holocaust and Genocide Studies <holocaust-education.dk/baggrund/antisemitisme.asp>.

[2] Shiku Smilovic, "We Are Free!" *Walk in My Shoes: Collected Memories of the Holocaust,* Museum of Family History <museumoffamilyhistory.com/wims-smilovic-buchenwald-liberation.htm>.

CHAPTER 8

Homeless Heroes

For people who had been scattered by the winds of war, the first priority was to try to locate the loved ones from whom they had been separated. Millions wondered if there was any hope of ever putting their families back together. By the end of World War II, 60 million people, military and civilian, were dead. Among them were 3 million Polish Jews and 2 million Polish Gentiles, more than 13 percent of Poland's total pre-1939 civilian population.

For Halina, still weak and trying to recover from her physical problems, the wait to find out about her family was excruciating. She was now in an American-run hospital in Germany, receiving the care she needed. Every so often a trickle of husbands came through the doors to embrace wives delirious with joy. Each day she prayed for her beloved Samuel, wondering if she would ever see him again.

The war had ripped families apart. Most survivors did not know who was dead or who was alive. The Germans had deported so many people and moved them around so much it was difficult to know how to look for someone. In many cases, it would take years—sometimes even a lifetime—for people to find one another. Halina was under no illusions about the Nazis. She knew what they were like and what had happened to Zygmund. In all likelihood, Samuel had perished.

It was her job now to rest and get well. As she lay in bed, the door swung open. When she looked up, her heart almost stopped. There, rushing toward her, was Samuel. The long nightmare of separation was over, and she was filled with the joy she had seen on the faces of other patients when their loved ones suddenly appeared.

"Oh, my darling!" she cried, as he swept her up in his arms. "I didn't know if I would ever see you again. But here you are!"

Samuel had been confined in a large prisoner of war camp in Woldenberg, Germany. (Today Woldenberg is Dobiegniew, Poland.) He was imprisoned with other high-ranking officers from the Warsaw Uprising who were brought there in October 1944. When the Russians liberated the camp in January 1945, the Russian commanders asked him to join the Russian army as an officer in their move to conquer Berlin. He declined, showing them his wounds and consequent inability to continue as a soldier.

As soon as he was released from the prison camp, Samuel began his long search for his wife. He knew Warsaw was the only place to begin. With no transportation and the city about 200 miles away, he started out on foot. Walking gave him time to do a lot of thinking, and he wondered not only about Halina's whereabouts, but whether she had even survived.

After their marriage in a ceremony that was necessarily a simple affair, their time together had been constantly disrupted by the fighting and seemingly endless months of captivity. Now he did not know if he would ever see her again. But he would not give up looking for her until he either found her or knew for certain she was dead.

Eventually, Samuel arrived in Warsaw where he went immediately to the apartment of Halina's mother. She was still living there, although it had been damaged by bombs during the Nazi occupation. After an emotional reunion, he began to ask questions. "Have you had any word from her?

Do you have any information about where she might be?"

The answer to both queries was no. "I only wish I knew," said her mother. "With my poor Zygmund dead, I have no one left. Please find her if you can. I long to see my child. But you cannot stay here in Warsaw," she warned her son-in-law. "It will be too dangerous for you."

When Samuel connected with a few friends who had served with him in the Polish Home Army, he learned what she had meant. To his great surprise and dismay, most of his fellow soldiers had been arrested by the Russians on information provided by a traitor who very likely had also named him as one of the intelligence officers working against Russia during the war.

So Samuel left Warsaw and headed south, eventually going as far as Czechoslovakia. He stopped at every former prison camp, asking for information about women prisoners who had been held there. Any shred of information he could find would help him in his search. The odds were heavily stacked against him. The war had displaced millions of people throughout Europe. Looking for one woman was like looking for a needle in a haystack. And with every country in shambles, there were few places where he could find anyone to help him.

For month after agonizing month, Samuel crisscrossed Poland and Germany in a fruitless search for Halina. Tired and discouraged, he paused one day to rest in a village square and was approached by a man wearing the red and white armband of the Polish Home Army. "Where are you going?" the man asked.

"Well, I can't tell you," Samuel replied wearily. "I am looking for my wife, who was in the army and taken prisoner by the Germans. I have no idea where she is."

"That's interesting," the soldier answered. "I've come a few days ago from Erfurt where I learned there was a prison camp for Polish women nearby. It was the Molsdorf encampment, and women were kept there until they were liberated by the Americans."

For the anguished husband, this information was like water from a desert stream. He was sure he had suddenly become the recipient of divine intervention. Adrenaline rushed throughout his exhausted body. This was the miracle he had prayed for so diligently. He would go there immediately. As he started out on what would become the last leg of his long and agonizing journey to find his wife, he was offered a ride from two soldiers in a Jeep. "Hop in," they told him. "We're on our way to Burg. We'll drop you there."

As they approached the town, he saw a small group of girls walking along the road. They were wearing the red and white armbands of the Home Army. Samuel asked the driver to pull over. "You were in a prison camp near here?" he asked the girls.

"Yes, we were at Molsdorf, not too far from here," replied one of them.

"Would you by any chance know a Halina Ostik?"

"Certainly. We were in the camp with her."

He could barely contain his excitement as he asked the big question: "Do you know where she is now?"

"Yes, she is at the American hospital in town. She has been quite ill. But when she sees you, I think her health will improve!"

She was alive. Relief flooded Samuel's soul, and he now knew he would finally see his wife. As he entered the facility, someone directed him to the room where she was resting, and their long and difficult separation came to an end.

৵

After a time for tears, nurses rushed into the room and began to dress Halina in street clothes. "This is not a time for you to be here," the head nurse exclaimed. "Go out and enjoy one another. Be careful for her legs," she told Samuel. "She has trouble walking. Go! Go!"

And go they did, to lodgings in a German house where they could be alone. They spent long hours filling each other in on where they had been, what they had done, and how they managed to survive the turbulent days when all there was time to think about was war and staying alive.

Now they faced another situation. Returning to Poland was out of the question. The Russians had replaced the Germans as occupiers, and the beleaguered Polish people were entering the dismal years of the harsh rule of Communism. Though Halina and Samuel longed to return, especially to be near Halina's mother, they had to flee. So after years of fighting the Germans in hopes of living in a free Poland, they were on the run again. But where were they to go?

They investigated the possibility of going to England. But they could not obtain the necessary permissions. For a while they lived in Holland, where they were welcomed. But the search continued for a permanent home where they could put down roots and begin life as a family. By now they knew that would not be as easy as they had hoped.

Samuel and Halina learned the unhappy truth that there is often an unfortunate twist in the aftermath of war. When the hard-fought struggles come to an end, those who continue to pay a price are usually the very people who fought and risked everything to win the victory. Few of the heroes from the brutal battles to save Europe from the Third Reich suspected that they would become casualties of another kind when the war ended. For the Polish, life did not return to normal. Freeing Poland of Hitler's brutal occupying force merely opened the door for the Russians.

Early after the war ended, some Poles wanted to launch an attack to drive the Soviet Union out. But they knew they would be going it alone. No help would be coming from Britain or America, who had made agreements with their then ally, Communist dictator Joseph Stalin. And the Home Army, which had answered to the supreme commander in London, had been all but destroyed.

At the Yalta Conference in February 1945, British Prime Minister Winston Churchill, U.S. President Franklin Roosevelt, and Stalin had sat down to decide how to divide oversight of postwar Europe. All agreed that Poland would be placed under Russian oversight on the promise that free elections would be held and a subsequent Polish government put in place.

However, promises made were not promises kept. Once control was in their hands, the Russians squelched free elections and failed to install a proper Polish government. In fact, to the dismay of Churchill and Roosevelt, all governments under Russian control were taken over by the Communists. From then on, Poland was closed to anyone who might be regarded as a potential threat to the Communist regime.

᙮

Knowing they could not return to Warsaw, Samuel and Halina began searching for a country that would take them in. After suffering through the bitter years of war fighting for Poland and freedom, they now found themselves homeless.

They were like vagabonds, moving from place to place in search of a nation that would allow them to settle there permanently.

One of their stops was Italy. There, in 1946, Halina gave birth to their first child, a daughter. Now they had three mouths to feed and no permanent place to live. Other stops were Wales and England. Some members of the Polish Resistance who had money moved to England and did quite well for themselves by opening businesses. But the Ostiks had no money; and due to their poor health, they were unable to work on the farms or in the quarries, which seemed to be the only jobs available. In Wales, Halina gave birth to their second daughter.

One day, while the family was in London, seven parcels arrived for them. They contained clothes and food for the girls. With them was a letter. Halina could hardly believe who had written it. It was from Victor Buksbazen, whom she remembered fondly as the young man who had accompanied her and Miss Pankerst to the resort by the Baltic when she was as a child.

Fluent in seven languages, Victor became a professor of Old Testament at the University of Warsaw but moved to England before the German occupation, which spared him the gruesome fate that befell most of his colleagues. In England he married and then immigrated to the United States, where he became the first executive director of The Friends of Israel, a Christian mission founded in Philadelphia, Pennsylvania, in 1938 to help Jewish people trying to flee Europe.

The Friends of Israel now was devoted to helping them recover from the Holocaust and reaching the world with the gospel. Through mutual friends, Victor had learned of Halina's whereabouts and wanted to help her. From then on, he corresponded with Halina and Samuel regularly, sending them parcels from time to time and money to help with the girls' education.

Everything he sent, they desperately needed. But what they needed still more was a permanent place to live. Their options were running out, and they were tired of being homeless.

Canada was attractive, but the £500 ($2,000 in 1945) required for entrance dashed their hopes. South Africa, New Zealand, and Australia were also closed to them. Only Polish soldiers who fought alongside the South Africans or the Aussies who fought in the British army were welcome.

After three years of being people without a country, good news finally arrived when they were in London. Argentina was open to them—no money required. So in 1948, with £2 in their pockets and two little daughters in tow, they joined 1,500 other immigrants aboard the Winchester Council steamer and rode the waves for four weeks, disembarking in Argentina:

> *After we arrived in the country, we felt as rich as lords as we walked through beautiful Buenos Aires with our £2 in pocket. We were not worried because we knew that our Father in heaven was in charge and taking care of us.*
>
> *And we were so happy that at long last, we were in a free land where no one would be cursing us, and there were no wire fences keeping us from the outside. That was all over now, and freedom was real.*

What the happy couple was not aware of was that their new land was also open to notorious war criminals who had escaped the Allied Nazi hunters. A neighbor might be German mass murderer Adolf Eichmann or another infamous Nazi. But all Halina and Samuel knew was that they were free. And that was enough.

Samuel's first job in Buenos Aires was not lucrative. When payday came, decisions had to be made. His 12 pesos a day were enough to pay the rent or buy food, but not to do both. Making ends meet was difficult. Somehow they made it through. Then good news came. Samuel returned from work one day with a big smile, waving an envelope in his hand. "My check from the army came today!"

It was money due him that had somehow been buried in bureaucracy before being found and forwarded. "This means we can buy some land and move out of here. They're selling plots of land north of Buenos Aires. I've seen the area. I think we can build a home and be very comfortable there," he told his wife.

The move would prove to be from poverty to primitive. There was only one dilapidated structure on the plot—a small shed made of bricks. The bricks became the foundation for the house, which initially consisted of two small rooms and a roof supported by a single strong beam. For flooring, Halina and Samuel compacted the dirt floor as well as they could with their feet.

With no money for furniture, they used a folding camp bed and made a plan to add a piece at a time until their little place was furnished. Until they could do better, empty fruit crates from the market were stacked for shelving and storage.

When they stood back to survey their handiwork, there wasn't a lot to write home about. At best, it was like a throwback to the pioneering days of the Old West in America. For Halina, it was a long, long way from the shaded glens of the plush resorts and retreats she had played in by the Baltic

Sea back in Poland. Those days were gone, banished from all but her memory. The little hut north of Buenos Aires was her reality, and she could not have been more content:

> *We at last had our own home. And I felt very rich and very happy. It was a new chapter. And I felt that it was the beginning I had dreamed of during all of the bleak, painful nights in the prison camps.*

Life was difficult but happy. Samuel frequently had to hold down two jobs in order to pay the bills and buy furnishings and basic materials to finish the house. He was out of bed at 3:30 A.M. to get to work at 7. Sometimes he didn't get home until 10 at night. When he came through the door, Halina was waiting for him with a lit lamp and a meal cooked on a gas stove. There was no electricity in the area. As she waited for her husband, she was on guard to see that the mice didn't beat Samuel to the food. They proved to be formidable opponents. As quickly as Halina and Samuel filled the mouse holes, the critters would gnaw their way through; and the contest would begin again.

But nothing really worried them. They were full of thanks and joy. "We loved one another deeply," Halina said, "and were a most happy family."

∽

Soon after Samuel arrived home from work one day, the wind began to pick up. As usual, Halina was waiting for him with supper as the darkness set in. She had prepared a special meal with meat on an outdoor charcoal grill. A pot of soup waited inside. As they walked back toward the house with the meat platter, a sudden gust of wind caught them by surprise. Without any warning, they had been struck by the first blows of a hurricane.

They immediately ran toward the door, but it slammed shut before them. Both panicked when they could not force it open. The strong wind coming through the windows was pinning the door to its frame. Inside were the girls, and Samuel worked frantically to get them out. To protect his wife, he pushed her to the side just as the wind began to tear the roof off the building. When the roof broke free, the pressure on the door subsided, and Samuel was able to reach the children and get them out of the house.

Unfortunately for Halina, she was in the wrong place at the wrong time. The roof's large support beam fell on her, pinning her to the ground. The pain in her chest was so excruciating she could hardly breathe. With herculean effort, Samuel moved the beam and pulled his mud-covered wife out from underneath the remnants of the roof.

He managed to carry her to the home of neighbors whose more substantial dwelling had fared better than theirs. The wife cleaned Halina up and placed her in one of the beds in their home. She was still having great pain and difficulty breathing, and everyone feared she had broken ribs that were piercing her lungs.

The next day, the doctor arrived. "You are a very fortunate young lady," he told her. "Because you are in your early thirties, your ribs did not break. They were just depressed into your lungs, but they did not pierce them. If that had happened, you would not be here talking to me today. Count yourself very lucky to have survived."

He may have thought her lucky, but Halina was certain her life was spared by the hand of the same loving Lord who had brought her through so much already.

I can't explain it, but when I was under the beam and suffered terrible pain, I also felt God's love surrounding me like a warm, comfortable blanket. I don't know how to express it. I felt His love all around me. I felt the sweetness and warmth of His presence.

Looking back on it now, I think I experienced a measure of what the martyrs must have felt when they were tortured. On the one hand, they felt pain. I, too, felt terrible pain. And at the same time, they must have experienced love and comfort.

It may sound strange for me to say this, but if I had to choose, I would choose to have this experience again. The reason is that during those awful moments under the beam, His love and presence were so tangible, so wonderful, that it deepened my walk with God in a way that would endure when the hurricane was far behind me.

Halina learned another lesson from the experience, as well. In her heart she yearned for her beloved Poland to be free from the yoke of the Communists. Perhaps she hoped the Americans would turn on the Russian occupiers and give her people back their country. Now, however, she felt that somehow God was caring for the people of Poland in the same way He had cared for her when she was unable to help herself. She knew in a deeper, more personal way that her trust should not be in politicians or armed forces, but in the Lord who had said through Isaiah the prophet, "For my thoughts are not your thoughts, neither are your ways my ways, saith the LORD. For as the heavens are higher than the earth, so are my ways higher than your ways, and my thoughts than your thoughts" (55:8–9).

It was best left to her God to direct the future, particularly because she would need His strength for what was coming.

CHAPTER 9

In God's Waiting Room

Life after the hurricane seemed to turn into a jumble of events that brought irreversible changes to the Ostik family. Not that rapid change was new to Halina. The war had taught her resiliency and how to cope with events as they occurred, both good and bad. Still, she had not fully recovered from the illness that left her in a permanent state of semi weakness. She had two young daughters to care for, and Samuel was often out of work because of the economic uncertainty and turmoil in Argentina under the government of Juan Perón.

However, times of testing frequently brought opportunities for spiritual growth. The Ostiks needed to find a church home. Their search brought them into close contact with many strong believers in Temperley, outside Buenos Aires, who had a fervent desire to obey the Lord and were good at extending warmth and friendship to newcomers. It was there that Samuel expressed a desire to be baptized. Since Halina had not been baptized by immersion, she felt she should join her husband.

Samuel asked the elder in charge of the ceremony for permission to speak in Polish to their girls and explain what baptism meant to him. He also wanted to tell them of his deepening relationship with the Lord, who had brought Halina and him through the trauma of war and into a place of safety where they could start a new life. They approached the service with a sense of excitement and anticipation.

When it came time for me to go into the water, I was reminded of Galatians 6:14: "But God forbid that

125

I should glory, save in the cross of our Lord Jesus Christ, by whom the world is crucified unto me, and I unto the world."

The words came so vividly that I was moved to feel that, at this moment, I was being liberated from the world that had always held so many attractions for me. Not in a bad way, but through things like science, theater, cinema, art, and social work. And as I came up out of the water, I was being liberated and was free to completely love the Lord, to serve Him, to be led by Him and enjoy all it meant to be close to Him.

This new dedication became the sustaining force in Halina's life. After returning home from their spiritual mountaintop experience, bad news arrived. The firm Samuel worked for was slated to close, and Samuel found himself out of a job again. The young family now faced several months of unemployment, with the only income being through an assortment of odd jobs that brought in a few pesos here and there. Their pressing financial distress led to a pattern of borrowing and repaying. It seemed their only option.

They would borrow from friends, perhaps 10 pesos (about $2), for food. When Samuel got work gardening, they would repay the loan. That is how they survived. One Sunday afternoon when they were reading the Bible, Halina found herself engrossed in the words of Romans 13, particularly verse 8: "Owe no man any thing, but to love one another: for he that loveth another hath fulfilled the law."

"Owe no man anything." The words came like a slap in the face. She felt that she and Samuel had been doing exactly the wrong thing in the eyes of the Lord. They were borrowing in order to eat. But they were committing a sin by doing so.

That day they decided there would be no more borrowed pesos. It was a huge decision, but there it was. They were going to stop borrowing and depend entirely on the Lord for their needs from day to day. Now they would have to tell their friends, mostly Polish immigrants like themselves, that they no longer would be borrowing, even though their friends were always more than happy to lend a few pesos.

Samuel and Halina knelt together and confessed their lack of trust. They told the Lord that whatever happened, they would not borrow money because they wanted to obey the Word and "owe no man any thing, but to love." So from that day, things took another turn. Samuel could no longer take the train into Buenos Aires in search of employment. There was no money for the fare.

Now, what to do? Looking over their supplies, Halina found flour, oil, gas for the cooker, and a few other items.

I decided to make noodles as the main dish. Though I had no eggs, I mixed flour and water then spooned it into boiling water. There was a piece of onion that I mixed with oil to add taste. For a salad, I went to the garden and pulled some bitter leaves. The Argentina people thought they were tasty and good for the blood. Not very appealing to my taste, but we did have a salad.

When we sat down for our first meal after the big decision to completely trust the Lord's care, Samuel laughed. "My dear, this is a meal fit for a king. Let's enjoy!" It was, in fact, a blessing that we didn't expect. That night, we went to bed and slept well, feeling that, in spite of what seemed like a hard place to be in, the Lord was in control, and we could rest.

The next day, Samuel was working in the garden and Halina was in the house tending to the children when she heard a loud knocking on the door. Startled, she opened it to see a rather rotund man who introduced himself as the president of the Polish Society and asked her to call her husband.

"I thought I'd never find you. I've been searching for you for two hours," he told her.

"I'm sorry for that," said Samuel. "As you well know by now, our house is rather isolated."

"That's neither here nor there at the moment," he replied. "The important thing is that I've found you, and I bring you some very good news. We have found a job for you, and you can start work immediately. How does that sound?"

After the man left, Samuel and Halina sat down and tried to absorb what had just transpired. "You know, Samuel," said Halina, "it was a very good thing that we were not found by the Polish Society sooner, because if he had arrived several days ago, we would not have learned the important lesson about trusting the Lord alone. Isn't it wonderful how we have been taught we do not need to trust even our friends' mercy when we are in need? Our wonderful Lord in heaven is our Father of mercy and comfort. How grateful we should be."

There they were, two World War II survivors who had walked through a valley of tears, mistrust, and doubts and lost nearly everything, including their country, relatives, and dearest friends. They lived as exiles in a tenuous situation in a strange land. Yet their simple and somewhat superficial understanding of "owe no man any thing" and their commitment to obey their Lord brought a blessing of incalculable proportion. It was confirmation that God was indeed with them, caring for them and guiding them. In a

Halina at age 2.

Halina at age 6, feeding a dove.

Polish Girl Guides. (Public Domain Source: en.wikipedia)

Halina and her Granny.

Warsaw before the war. (FOI Image Archive)

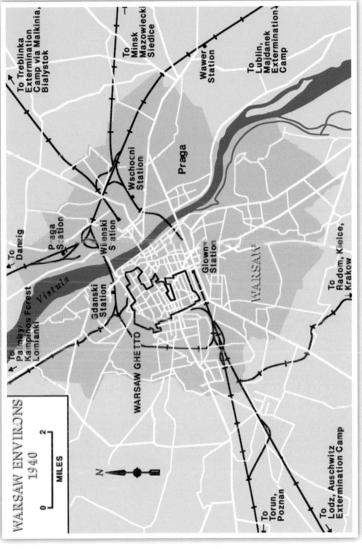

This maps shows how trains from Warsaw led to extermination camps during World War II.
(United States Holocaust Memorial Museum, Washington, DC)

Jewish children in the Warsaw Ghetto. (United States Holocaust Memorial Museum Yad Vashem
Photo Archives, courtesy of Guenther Schwarberg © copyright United States Holocaust Memorial Museum)

German soldiers lead Jews captured during the Warsaw Ghetto uprising to the assembly point for deportation.

German soldiers burn the Warsaw Ghetto to the ground. (National Archives and Records Administration, College Park Instytut Pamieci Narodowej Sovfoto/Eastfoto © copyright Public Domain)

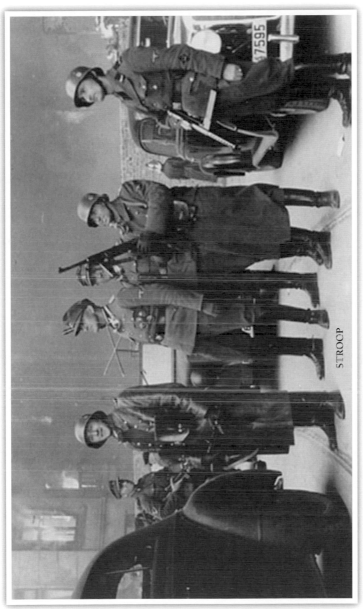

Jürgen Stroop watches as the Warsaw Ghetto burns. (The United States Holocaust Memorial Museum © copyright Public Domain)

The Great Synagogue on Tlomackie Street, before and after it was blown up. (www.holocaustresearchproject.org)

Women prisoners in Ravensbrook concentration camp. (www.holocaustresearchproject.org)

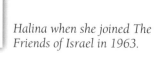

Halina when she joined The Friends of Israel in 1963.

Halina (left) and Anna Cieślar in 1976. Anna joined The Friends of Israel two years later.

Halina in 1990.

The "ghosts of Muranów."
(Anna Cieślar/FOI Image Archive)

The symbol for "Poland is fighting."
(Krzysztof Machocki [halibutt.pl] CC-BY-SA)

Halina in 1991.

Halina and a Holocaust survivor.

Nathan Rapoport's Monument to the Ghetto Heroes in Warsaw.

In her office in Warsaw in 2000.

Halina after sharing in a church in 1998.

Halina with FOI International Ministries Director David M. Levy.
(FOI Image Archive)

The Friends of Israel's children's camp in Poland. The adults in the front row are (from left) the author, Elwood McQuaid; Halina; and Zvi Kalisher, a Polish Jewish Holocaust survivor who has served with The Friends of Israel in Jerusalem since the 1950s. (FOI Image Archive)

way that can only be understood by others who have trod the same path, they experienced the truth of Psalm 27:10: "When my father and my mother forsake me, then the LORD will take me up."

⸉

The next months were happy days filled with work for Samuel. Halina was content to be a joyful keeper of the home. But slowly it became obvious things were not right with Samuel. He slipped downhill physically until he told his concerned wife that his pain had increased to the point that he needed to go to the hospital. At the hospital, the doctors decided they needed to perform exploratory surgery to diagnose his problem.

Outside the operating room, Halina anxiously waited for the verdict.

"I'm afraid I have bad news for you," the surgeon began. "Your husband has cancer of the liver, a very serious disease."

"What can be done to treat him?"

"Not much," the surgeon replied. "His condition is incurable. And I can tell you that, in all probability, you will have him for two more months. What you can do in the meantime is make him comfortable. We will do our best to manage the pain."

Halina sat frozen, tears streaming down her cheeks. The thought of life without Samuel was unbearable. It was beyond her ability to take it all in. In the recovery room, she put on a brave face. "What have the doctors told you?" she asked.

"It's not good news," he replied. "They will do all they can, but they were not happy with the outcome. The only thing that was hopeful in the least was that they will not be doing any more surgery."

From their brief conversation, Halina could not be sure how much he knew about the seriousness of his condition. Determined not to expose her anguish before her dying husband, she never cried in his presence. For the precious weeks remaining of their time together, she kept a nearly constant vigil by his bedside.

Her grief was tremendous. There was only one place she could go with it: to her heavenly Father. She asked Him to calm her and give her His perfect peace, as He had promised. She knew her husband loved the Lord and would go to heaven. He had accepted the sacrifice of Christ on the cross for the forgiveness of sin, and he was assured of everlasting life. All Halina could do now was wait and pray that God would control Samuel's suffering.

As she awaited the inevitable, the doctors increased the morphine dosage until Samuel slept for long intervals. Two weeks before he passed into eternity, he told Halina there was something he wanted her to know. "I can already see Christ waiting at the end of a long road, which I still have to cover before I will be with Him. And then I will be in His presence forever," he told her. "The Lord also told me that I should be at peace for you and the children. He will take care of you." Halina never forgot his words.

> *Those words were very precious to me, a reminder of the Lord's Word in Deuteronomy: "Be strong and of a good courage, fear not, nor be afraid of them; for the LORD thy God, he it is that doth go with thee; he will not fail thee nor forsake thee" [31:6].*

A few days later, he roused from his sleep and took my hand. He looked very tired. I asked him, "Samuel, do you rest in the Lord?" He returned a weak smile and replied, "You know that I do."

It was about two in the morning when he slipped away, and I was left by his bedside alone.

Now it was time for tears.

∽

The days that followed Samuel's death were filled with uncertainty. What the future held was a complete mystery to Halina, whose preparation for a meaningful occupation had been cut short by the war. Her days as a soldier dodging and fighting Nazis were not a ticket to a career she could rely on to support herself and two daughters under age seven. She thought about nursing. That had been the one part of her training through the Girl Guides that might hold some promise. It had enabled her to tend to the wounded in the war.

"Why not consider giving English lessons?" asked a friend. "There is a great need for English teachers in Argentina."

"But do you think my English is good enough?" asked Halina.

"Yes, it most certainly is. Go into a school and listen to what passes for English instruction there. You will be convinced Argentinian English instructors are far from excellent, or even what one would consider good. What I suggest is that you begin by giving private lessons. That will give you the chance to try it out and see how it goes."

Halina decided to take her friend's advice. Soon she had several students and was earning enough to stabilize her income. Before long she received an invitation to teach at one of the local schools. Her time as an English teacher provided a bridge between Samuel's passing and God's plan for her future.

For the young, new widow, every day held so many challenges that Poland and the past seemed a distant memory. Keeping her home and two daughters together was all she could handle as she tried to adjust to life as a single mother and sole provider.

One day mail arrived postmarked from America. As she opened the envelope and unfolded the letter, she found herself reading a note from her dear friend Victor Buksbazen. He had learned of Samuel's death; and though he knew nothing of Halina's financial straits, he had enclosed precisely the amount of money she needed to cover a month of living expenses and help dig a well and install a pump to bring water into her home.

Eventually, life began to return to normal. Halina accepted an invitation from a mission agency to work among the Indians in Argentina. She ministered among them for a number of years and developed a strong bond with the tribal people.

During her time in Argentina, she was reading The Friends of Israel's magazine, *Israel My Glory*, and learning what the Lord was doing among the Jewish people. She loved her work among the Indians, but she also had a great love for Jewish people and quietly thought to herself, "What a pity that I am not Jewish. If I were a Jewess, perhaps I could join the mission and minister to the Jewish people. But since I was not brought up in a Jewish home, I really know very little about Jewish tradition and Jewish thought. No, it could never happen."

Then in 1961, another letter arrived from Dr. Buksbazen.

This one was different from all the others. It contained an invitation to join the Bible-teaching staff of The Friends of Israel.

Immediately, my mind was flooded with reasons why it was not possible. But then, through extensive correspondence, Victor related reasons why he did not agree. It seemed that to every objection I raised, he had a perfectly reasonable answer.

I did have a good knowledge of the Jewish people, he argued. And I had something of great value in working with Jewish people that others did not. I had passed through the same struggles as they during the war. Therefore, I knew firsthand about the terrible agonies they suffered. Perhaps, he concluded, my greatest qualification was that of a heart full of compassion for His people.

As I sat, letter in hand, thinking about what I had read, my mind went back to my childhood in Warsaw and seeing the faces of those Jewish children running out to school. And how pale and gaunt their faces were because they didn't have the right things to eat. Yes, my compassion as a child had grown with me and helped me to do dangerous things to help save Jewish children and families from the Warsaw Ghetto during the war.

Victor was right about that, but I still had some doubts.

As if this dilemma were not enough, there was something else. Halina had answered God's call to minister among the Indians of Argentina. She loved them; she loved the work. How could it be that God would suddenly change things and send her in another direction?

After spending serious time in prayer, she began to understand things a little more. Though drawn by her commitment to the tribal people, she always felt there would come a day when God would return her to Poland. Perhaps Victor's offer was how that would come about. Now time was becoming of the essence. Halina had told Victor she would give him her answer in two weeks. And though she was praying, the days were passing with no answer from God.

One day I said to the Lord, "Please speak to me through your Word. I have to know your will." With that, I opened the Bible at random, and my eyes fell on Matthew, chapter 10. "Well, what answer could be here?" I thought. As I was about to turn the page and look some other place, I was impressed to stop and read before going on. I didn't read long before I came to verse 6, and I was stunned as I stared at the words: "But go, rather, to the lost sheep of the house of Israel."

I immediately fell on my knees. I repeated over and over, "Yes, Lord, I will do it." When I stood up, I was absolutely sure that this was a new call. The turmoil was ended, and I had peace. The Lord would not forsake my precious Indians but would provide others to carry on the work. And even though I parted from them, they would never leave my heart or be beyond the reach of my prayers.

I sat down almost immediately to write Dr. Buksbazen with my agreement to join The Friends of Israel ministry. As I wrote my testimony, I was deeply appreciative of the peace I now felt. I can say that God's peace and my conviction of the right decision have never diminished.

Although her decision was made, Halina pondered how

she, a Gentile, could relate to Jewish people. She wondered if Victor fully understood what she considered to be her disadvantage. In reality, however, she had two distinct advantages: (1) a wealth of experiences that set her apart from the vast majority of Christians and (2) a personal intimacy with her Lord that made her teachable. It was on the second point that she received a fundamental readjustment in her thinking.

> *Always before, I had read and studied the Bible as if it were written for my personal growth and comfort. Now I was impressed to read it as a new Book, paying a special attention to what the Scriptures said, especially about and to the Jewish people. What I found very quickly was what I can best describe as a revolution in my thinking.*
>
> *As I read, I found that it was a Book with much written specifically for Israel and God's promises to His people. I took colored pencils, and as I read the Bible from beginning to end, I would mark with a red pencil all of the places in which I could gain an understanding of His love for the Jewish people. Among the things I discovered was there were so many statements that were not known to me. A good example is in Isaiah 40, where the Lord says, "Comfort ye, comfort ye my people, saith your God," and also, when Jewish people were dying in the streets, "What shall I equal to thee, that I may comfort thee; . . . who can heal thee?" [Lam. 2:13]. I interpreted these verses in a personal way, to know that my mission was to comfort and console the people who had suffered so dreadfully for so long.*
>
> *With a green pencil I would underline beautiful prophecies about the future blessings for Israel*

> *when the Messiah comes, especially how the land will blossom, even the desert; the trees will "clap their hands" [Isa. 55:12], which means be fruitful and well cared for. At the center of all was Jerusalem and the future glory it will know under Messiah's rule.*
>
> *Then, with a blue marker, I underlined all of the passages referring to His Second Coming—His coming again in glory to reign over His people and the earth.*

One passage in particular struck a note deep in her heart. It took her back to the tumultuous days of the Warsaw uprising.

> *When I read Isaiah 62:10, I found a command to "gather out the stones" when building up Jerusalem in the coming days of her glory in peace and security. I thought of our taking up the stones of the streets in Warsaw to build barriers sheltering us from the guns of the Nazis.*
>
> *But I also was struck by the thought that for centuries, so-called Christians had built barriers around the Jewish people by persecuting and despising them as "Christ-killers." The barriers were so intense that Jewish people couldn't see the Lord Jesus.*

In her pursuit of God's Word and what it says about Israel and the Jewish people, Halina received divine confirmation of the unity of Scripture. She discovered that interpreting the Bible in its literal, historical, and cultural context revealed to her that God's program for Israel did not end when the New Testament era began. Everything the Lord has promised Israel, He will fulfill. She saw clearly that God would never replace His beloved people with the church; He has a divine program for each of them. He loves the church, and He loves Israel. His heart is big enough to love them both.

Halina sought the truth with an open heart and mind, and the Holy Spirit educated her using God's Word. The Jewish people had been battered and decimated. Fifteen years earlier, they had staggered out of the most horrible, genocidal epic the world had known. And they desperately needed to know how much God loved them. Halina could be trusted to deliver the right message at the right time.

God had written the way to the future through the prophets and Jesus. Jesus did not come to Earth on a mission to turn Jews into Gentiles. He came to die in their place as a final sacrifice for sin so that a holy God could extend forgiveness for eternity.

Hitler was not a Christian, nor were the Nazis. They were merely Gentiles, men like Jürgen Stroop, who persecuted true believers and dreamt of refashioning the world in their own godless image. They did not reflect the historic Jesus, the Jesus of the Bible, who loves Israel and Jewish people. Rather, they reflected the demonic side of life, which is controlled by Satan and his hatred of all things God loves And they will spend eternity with Satan in the Lake of Fire, where they will reap what they sowed (Rev. 20).

Halina had a message of hope for everyone who had suffered so much at the hands of Hitler's Third Reich: Faith in Israel's Messiah, the Savior of the Gentiles, is the common path to forgiveness of sin and eternal life.

At 42 years old, Halina was about to start a new life. As she entered the first Jewish shop on a street in Buenos Aires, she carried the message of God's everlasting love—through her words and from her heart.

CHAPTER 10

No Sermons, Please

Halina was somewhat apprehensive about how she would be received in the Jewish shops along the streets of Buenos Aires. In her handbag were special copies of the New Testament that contained prophecies of the Messiah. She was almost muttering to herself as she approached the first shop.

I thought, "If they realize, those people to whom I am going to talk and present a New Testament, that I am a Christian and I am Polish, that I came from the country of the Holocaust, they may spit on me and drive me out of their store." Many Jewish people believe that Christian hatred was at the bottom of their troubles. Some even believe that Adolf Hitler was a Christian. "Well, if that's the worst thing that can happen, I will just have to take it," I decided. After all, what so-called Christians did to them was much worse than pushing them out a door. I'm here to show them the love of Christ, and that there are many of us who would never hurt or persecute Jewish people.

But I quickly learned that it was not going to happen. They were almost always very polite and willing to talk. I would begin the conversation by saying how happy I was about the things that were happening in Israel. I told them how happy I was that Israel exists again as an independent state and that the deserts are beginning to blossom and that trees were growing again on the mountains of Israel. The towns, which were destroyed centuries ago, are being rebuilt. And that most of all I am happy that the Messiah is coming to Israel. It is He who will finally put everything right. In the meantime, He is protecting them in spite of all of their enemies.

These were all things that we shared in common. When I offered them the New Testament I brought, they accepted it politely. Most would put it under the counter to read later, I would hope. My prayer was that perhaps when the shopkeeper was alone and out of sight of other people, he would have curiosity and start reading it. Maybe it would provoke him to become interested in the genealogy of Jesus of Nazareth and find that Jesus was a Jew, a descendant of King David. Then maybe in time, the Lord would open his heart to the Messiah, and we would meet again in heaven.

Most touching to me were those who were from Poland themselves or had parents who came from there. They would ask me question after question about Poland and what it was like before the war. There was no hatred, but a kind of kindred feeling toward another Pole, even if she was a goy [Yiddish and Hebrew for "Gentile"].

But after that first day in the shops, I learned something that I had not suspected before. I was in a shop talking to a man who professed no interest in the Bible, telling me it was only a book written by men. That changed when a lady came in and joined the conversation. She warned that her priest said it was wrong to read the Bible at all. Then the shopkeeper spoke up and began defending a person's reading of the Book. I left impressed by the belief that deep down in every Jewish heart, especially if a person had godly parents, there is a deep respect for the Bible.

As I met many more people over the next two years, I found that we were not meeting as adversaries, but as those who had much in common. I must say in all honesty, that this was a necessary time for me to learn so much more about Jewish people. As I prepared to leave Argentina and return to Poland, it would be like I had been two years in university, studying the people who are so close to the heart of our Lord. They were, perhaps, in a place so bitterly torn in spirit that I could bring a deepened sense of devotion to Christ and compassion for the Jewish people.

As it turned out, it was indeed God's plan to bring Halina home to Poland. But the process was fraught with obstacles. After the Allies ridded the country of the Nazis, they looked on benignly as Communism took over and dominated Polish social and political life. Communism would not fall and set Poland free until 1989.

From the outset, the Roman Catholic Church was the primary target of the anti-God, socialist regime. In the early 1950s, the Communist war against religion manifested itself through the activities of the secret police. Hundreds of dissenting Polish religious leaders were arrested and tortured. Active Christians lived with trepidation and caution, never knowing who was looking over their shoulders.

Halina knew all this. But she also knew she would finally be reunited with her dear mother and at long last be back in her own country. So she left Argentina in 1963 and set sail for Poland.

After four weeks at sea, the ship docked in Gdansk. A

relative of Samuel's was waiting to pick her up and take her to Warsaw to see her mother, whom she had not seen in six years. In 1957, three years after Samuel died, her mother finally managed to obtain a passport from the Communists, allowing her to go to Argentina. By then Mrs. Peszke was 76 years old and had not seen her daughter for 13 long years. She stayed with Halina two years before returning to Poland.

When Halina entered her mother's flat, she was greeted by a tired-looking 82-year-old woman on crutches who hardly resembled the mum who had taken her on shopping trips in Warsaw and distributed food and clothing to the poor. Those days were a lifetime ago. But none of that seemed to matter at the moment. As soon as they saw each other, they locked in a joyful embrace that erased the many yesterdays of separation. Halusia was finally home.

⸎

Victor Buksbazen had told Halina, "In Poland you may minister to both Jews and Gentiles because they both need the Messiah." His words were prophetic because she found both had immense needs. Before the Holocaust, Poland had 3.3 million Jewish people, the largest Jewish population in Europe. By the 1950s, only 45,000 were left—and they were still reeling from the trauma of what they had been through. Most lived in a state of near paranoia as they tried to put their lives back together. Many had lived with false identities for years and were still wary of what might happen if they were identified as Jewish.

It was almost as though the tattered remains of the Jewish people had emerged from total darkness, blinking at the light of a strange world. Their perception that "Christianity" had tried to destroy them made them understandably suspicious of anyone and anything deemed Christian. And who could blame them? In her early days back in Poland, Halina found herself focusing on God's words in Isaiah 40:1: "Comfort ye, comfort ye my people, saith your God." And that was what she intended to do.

Undoing the damage falsely done in the name of Christ would take time and an enormous amount of patience and understanding. But with God, all things are possible. Halina wanted the Jewish people of Poland to know that true friends of Israel existed and loved them. But she also knew that fact would have to be demonstrated through action, not merely through words.

The churches presented quite another problem. They suffered from a severe lack of understanding about Jewish people, and they comprehended even less about the importance of the State of Israel. They did not grasp God's eternal plan for the Jewish people or the church, and latent anti-Semitism astonishingly still lingered in some quarters. The Roman Catholic Church did not officially rescind its teaching that the Jewish people were "Christ-killers" until Vatican Council II of 1965. The absurd notion that the Jews were even partially guilty of bringing the Holocaust upon their own heads had not been completely washed out of the culture. Although Halina certainly did not feel qualified to address these huge problems, few people had been more thoroughly prepared for the task.

Victor Buksbazen had given Halina a number of names of Jewish survivors who needed the material assistance The Friends of Israel could provide, as well as the ministry of the love of Christ. Halina spent many hours listening to these survivors relate the details of the tragedies they had endured. In every instance, they seemed to find comfort in sharing their grief with an understanding friend. One woman to whom she ministered was considered mentally ill. But the condition was completely the fault of the Nazis.

> *When she sensed that her situation was deteriorating, she would go into a mental institution. After weeks of treatment, she would return home until the next episode. Her illness was a direct result of the atrocities inflicted by the Gestapo because she was a Jewess. They had broken her and framed a permanent mental affliction from which she would never escape.*
>
> *As I listened, I wondered how many thousands of other broken people there were who, although they escaped the gas chambers, would never be rid of the permanent scars inflicted during the war.*

Then there was the immense privilege of meeting those who were true heroes—true Bible-believing Christians who had risked everything to save Jewish people from the Germans. It took a special type of individual to value another's life as precious as one's own. Each time Halina met one of these people, she was encouraged and assured that God always places His people in every circumstance; and through Him, they will be strong no matter what the cost.

Among God's people during the Holocaust was Stephan who, with his wife, saved the lives of many Jewish people. One of them was a notable Jewish believer in Christ, Rachmiel Frydland, who was high on the list of people wanted by the Gestapo. In hiding Frydland, Stephan did what even the members of Frydland's own church refused to do. His own church had asked Frydland to stop attending because the Nazis ordered that Jews should be expelled from the churches. To bolster its position, Frydland's church used the Scripture that commands people to be subject to the authorities over them. So Frydland left his church. After hiding in cemeteries, deserted churches, and at times sneaking in and out of the Ghetto, Rachmiel found comfort in the home of the courageous couple.

Stephan and his wife also fed Jewish women who were hiding in the attic of a nearby house. Despite the fact they had very little food, every day they would take soup, bread, and whatever else they could find to feed the women. They knew if they were discovered, they would be killed. But they chose to obey God rather than wicked men and, in so doing, became the reason why some Jewish people made it through the horrors of the Holocaust.

෴

"You know, of course, that we do not allow women to preach sermons in our pulpits," a friendly Baptist pastor told Halina.

"Well, I don't preach sermons," she replied. "I just tell the people what is on my heart and what I have learned through the Bible and through my experiences with the Jewish people."

"Then that's all right. You may have a few minutes to talk to the people at our Thursday night prayer service," he told her.

The exchange between Halina and the pastor was the result of something remarkable that Halina had never expected. He had heard of her messages to a group of 15 women who had met daily in a home in Warsaw while the men attended a pastors' conference. One day while she was speaking on the judgments of God, there was a knock on the door. Her host opened it to a group of about 40 preachers who were taking a break from the conference. Somewhat embarrassed by their presence, Halina continued teaching nonetheless. When the meeting was over, many of the pastors asked if she would come to their churches and speak. That women's meeting opened the door for what would become Halina's extensive ministry in churches.

After Halina had spoken for some time at the Baptist pastor's Thursday night prayer service, she glanced at her watch to discover that she had gotten somewhat carried away. Her "few minutes" had turned into 30. "Oh my!" Halina declared, somewhat embarrassed. "I've spoken far too long. I'll sit down."

But the pastor raised his hand in protest. "Time is unlimited," he called out. "Go on. Go on." After another 15 minutes, she closed out her talk. Then the pastor approached with a request. "Could you continue each evening until Sunday?"

He then announced to the congregation that Halina would be speaking every evening, which gave her the opportunity to share her love and God's plan for the Jewish people. For the next 13 years, she tirelessly brought her message to the churches. Rarely did she initiate the visit. Pastors and congregations got in touch with her, eager to hear of God's love and grace that countered the hatred and discrimination they had lived with during the days of the Third Reich.

Though she was free to speak, she knew the Communist government planted informers in every service to listen for anything they deemed politically subversive. Though Halina was free in Christ, she still was not free in Poland.

Without realizing it, though, Halina was laying the groundwork for a ministry that would endure far beyond her expectations. She had become a trustworthy voice for the Lord and the State of Israel and aided in the spiritual growth of believers by preparing them to participate in the work of the ministry. What began with 15 women in a Warsaw living room set the stage for a ministry in Poland and an international outreach for years to come. Over the years she spoke in more than 40 churches.

Though God had called her to minister to the Jewish people, and her heart was yearning to do so, she was accomplishing much in the churches. And there was still more to do.

Brother Andrew and Corrie ten Boom

The Nazis and then the Communists had done their work in destroying the churches of Poland. Parts of the country had no evangelical churches at all. Led by the Holy Spirit, some brave people undertook the task of traveling to these areas to plant churches and distribute gospel booklets. It was a dangerous enterprise because anyone found with Bibles, New Testaments, or other forms of Christian literature was forced to give everything to the Communist authorities and possibly face dire consequences.

Even so, these believers were not easily intimidated, discouraged, or dissuaded from evangelizing. Many of them had served in the Resistance. So they devised a way to prevent their literature from being confiscated. They carried large backpacks of materials into the forest and hid them there, taking only a few pieces of literature when they entered a town. If confronted by police, they would give up their stock and then return to the forest to retrieve more gospel booklets.

In the town of Kielce, two determined young men who were aware of what life in Poland had been like under the Nazis distributed hundreds of booklets. During the war, the Nazis had purged Kielce's entire Jewish population. It was only after the Holocaust that a small band of Jewish survivors came back to the town in an attempt to return to a place of fond memories before Hitler's takeover.

Unfortunately, the Jews fared little better under Stalin. On July 4, 1946, a pogrom (government-sanctioned killing spree) against the Jewish community in Kielce took 40 lives. In later years, academics studying the massacre said the instigators were the Communist security forces. The pogrom sent a message to all anti-Communists that if they defied authority in any way, including by evangelizing, they would risk severe punishment.

That's precisely what happened to one of the men, Alfred, who distributed literature in Kielce. Though repeatedly picked up by police, Alfred was convinced his work in the town was God's call on his life. So he continued. Finally, police arrested him, jailed him, tortured him, and beat him within an inch of his life. Then they presented him with a passport and demanded he leave the country.

When Alfred arrived in West Germany, he was taken directly to a hospital. Years later, the people who had succeeded in establishing a number of churches in Kielce credited their efforts to the impact the sacrificial ministry of Alfred and his companions had made in their lives.

Like her friend Alfred, Halina did not hesitate to do her part. Despite the danger, she chose to obey God rather than those suppressing truth and faith in Him. When Netherlands-born Andrew van der Bijl (Brother Andrew) came to Warsaw in 1955, he saw Poland's deplorable spiritual condition and became burdened for the people there and everywhere behind the Iron Curtain (the 15 Eastern European countries bound to the Soviet Union by Communist Russia).

Consequently, he dedicated his life to ministering to the needs of churches under Communist domination. His work led to the founding of the Open Doors organization. And because of his untiring efforts to bring Bibles and Christian literature into Iron Curtain countries, Brother Andrew became known as "God's Smuggler."

Halina did not hesitate to help Brother Andrew get Bibles and Christian materials into the hands of Polish believers. Their first contact came when a Baptist pastor asked her to translate for Andrew when he came to speak in a church.

I loved translating for him because it was easy to do so for someone so obviously filled with the Holy Spirit. I felt that I didn't need to think of the words. They just seemed to flow out of me as he addressed the congregation. During this time we became good friends and decided that we would cooperate in delivering Bibles to people in Poland.

It wouldn't be without risk because if the authorities found stashes of Bibles and books in my apartment, there would be a heavy price to pay. To see to it this didn't happen, the Russian Bibles and Polish Christian literature were delivered in different ways that would not establish a pattern that someone would detect. We did it mostly at night, with the books carried into my flat in heavy suitcases. As quickly as possible, we would put them under the bed and wherever we could find places to hide them. We knew, of course, that if the secret police would raid the building, they would be discovered. So my young friends who were working with me would take the books out and distribute them as quickly as possible.

Only in heaven will we know how many people came to faith in Christ or were helped and instructed through the ministry of Brother Andrew and those of

> *us who worked with him. I do know that thousands of Bibles, books, and literature were put into the hands of people who needed the truth and comfort of the Word.*

Among Brother Andrew's closest friends was the Dutch heroine Corrie ten Boom, who became his traveling companion on many projects and speaking engagements. Her profound influence emanated from her deep Christian faith, which led her family in Holland to hide Jewish people from the Nazis at great personal sacrifice. The story became legendary through Corrie's best-selling book, *The Hiding Place,* later made into a film. The Ten Booms' willingness to defy the Nazis ultimately cost four members of the family their lives. However, they are credited with saving more than 800 Jewish people from perishing in the death camps.

Halina first met Corrie in Argentina before she and her daughters returned to Poland. After reading Corrie's 1954 book, *Prisoner and Yet,* depicting her life in the Ravensbruck women's prison camp in Germany, Halina felt a strong sense of identity with her.

Ravensbruck was notorious for its ill treatment of women. Between 1939 and 1945, some 130,000 passed through the camp. The final estimate of survivors was between 15,000 and 32,000. Among those who did not survive was Betsie, Corrie's sister. Although the Nazis brought prisoners to the facility from all over occupied Europe, most of the inmates were from Poland. So when Corrie visited Argentina, she was drawn to Polish women who, in one way or another, shared her wartime experiences.

Halina was the first to invite Corrie to address a group of Polish believers in the church she attended in Buenos Aires.

I think Corrie, who was accustomed to speaking to hundreds of people, was shocked when she stood before our little gathering of only 20 people. But she spoke to 20 with the same passion she would have had before filled auditoriums. We were enraptured as we listened to her tell of her experiences as a prisoner of war and later as a free woman.

As I translated her message, I prayed that someday I would have the privilege of doing the same thing for her when I returned to Poland. What had touched hearts so deeply in Argentina would be even more of an encouragement and blessing to people in Poland who had lived through the same perils.

Halina's prayers were answered when Corrie came to Poland. As had been true in Argentina, Halina was her translator. People were enthralled by the message about her experiences during and after the war. By then, many young people needed to be educated about how evil the Nazis were and how difficult life had been during the occupation. Corrie ten Boom had travelled extensively and was an international figure who captured their attention.

But she was somewhat taken aback by the reticence of the Polish congregations to react to some of the amusing stories that were so popular with other audiences. Halina explained that it was not because the stories were not appreciated, but that in Eastern Europe people were taught that laughing in church was not acceptable. Eastern Europeans were rather serious and much preferred being moved to tears than smiles, which demonstrated the gulf between the cultures of Eastern and Western Europe at the time.

Yet Corrie's presence and inspiring ministry brought light to many, many people. It also did a great deal to help Christians appreciate the Jewish people and teach them the obligation to reach out to them with a healing message of love.

There was no question that Halina was making a lasting impact in the churches where she spoke. She was taking advantage of the doors God was opening. But still, she had a growing sense of uneasiness. God had called her to minister among the Jewish people. And though she knew the church ministry was important, her heart was longing to grow closer to those so near to the heart of God.

She couldn't help but remember that Victor Buksbazen had told her she would be free to minister to both Gentiles and Jews in Poland. She had, at least in some measure, met the first part of Victor's challenge. Now, she concluded, it was time to begin to do what she could to tackle the second part—to reach out to Jews. After all, that's what she had been teaching people to do since she returned to her country. It was time to concentrate her personal energies on ministering to God's Chosen People.

CHAPTER 11

The Farm and Beyond

During her 13 years ministering in the churches, Halina developed the ability to serve as a type of bridge between the Polish church and Western believers who came to offer their services. During the Cold War, Communist-ruled Eastern Europe was in a state of paranoia when it came to messages going out to the West. The Soviet propaganda machine ground out word that people under their control were living in freedom when the truth was exactly the opposite.

Halina had an interesting view of these years of ministry.

The proper Jewish work started after those 13 years. I remembered that [the biblical patriarch] Joseph was 13 years in prison. That's how I felt. Thirteen years not able to reach out to the Jewish people, except those very few.

But down deep I knew that, like Joseph, those years of training were necessary because they were actually all preparation for future service.

Polish pastors were in a precarious situation. If they told their visitors the truth about the Communist oppression, the visitors would in turn tell the truth to their churches when they returned home. That was not the message the Communists wanted to see spread through overseas publications and broadcasts, which were all closely monitored by their intelligence agencies. If such news got out, the Polish congregations would feel the repercussions. So pastors put on a good face and took care that they did not expose their guests to information that would jeopardize the Polish believers.

Halina was in a unique situation. She had been reared in Poland but lived for years in the West. The combination gave her the ability to understand and relate with sensitivity to both cultures. She would take visitors into her home and explain to them the true situation for Christians and their churches under Communist rule. She made certain they understood the great harm that would be done if the information became public in the West and got back to authorities in the Eastern Bloc.

Simple things, such as giving a tract to a person on the street, had to be done carefully. Christians had to be sure no one was walking behind them or could see what they were doing. The government strictly controlled and monitored all printing and publishing. An organization could print only one book a year, which meant placing a number of books under a single cover.

One unfortunate pastor accused of running afoul of the printing rules was summoned to police headquarters, interrogated, threatened, and bullied before being released with a stern warning. He was told that if any more allegations were brought to police attention, the church would be closed, its magazine shut down, and its privilege to print one book a year revoked.

Many Western believers who visited learned what it meant to live in constant fear of one's own government. They began to understand somewhat that in every venue, there were government informers who listened for anything that deviated even slightly from what the authorities permitted. To some Westerners, their experience in Poland became a wakeup call to cherish and guard the precious freedom they had in the West—freedom their brethren in other parts of the world were denied.

⁓

The time had come for Halina to turn to ministry among her beloved Jewish people. One of her first steps was to direct Anna, a young colleague, to take a survey of Christian attitudes toward Jewish people. The survey asked four questions:

1. What is your attitude toward the Jewish people?

2. What is the attitude of the people who surround you toward the Jewish people?

3. Do you pray for the Jewish people?

4. Do you see any biblical reasons to pray for the Jewish people?

In all, 150 people participated. Halina received responses from ordinary individuals, church members, and young people attending winter camps. The answers were varied. Most described their attitude as good. However, when it came to the attitudes of their acquaintances, the responses tended to be "Many are negative."

On the prayer query, some saw no reason to pray specifically for Jewish people. One person said, "Yes, I did pray once, after a sermon." Most telling were the answers to question four. All 150 people, with the one exception, replied that they saw no biblical reason to pray for Jesus' Jewish brethren.

The lone positive answer came from someone who had heard a message from the pulpit that had stirred the individual's heart to pray for God's Chosen People. In analyzing the survey's results, Halina came to an obvious conclusion: People in the pews were not being taught from God's Word about the Jewish people.

Now her challenge was to prepare Bible studies for churches, helping them to teach biblical truth about Israel. A pastor, who was himself Jewish and had traveled to Israel, made a series of slide presentations based on his journey. Halina used his slides to complement her written studies, and God began a work to change attitudes among many Polish Christians and impress on them their obligation to appreciate Israel's place in His plan and "pray for the peace of Jerusalem" (Ps. 122:6).

Years later, Halina thought back on that simple survey. "If we could go back to the same people today and ask the same questions," she said, "I think there would be very different answers to Anna's questions."

༄

Before the war, Warsaw was a city of synagogues. An estimated 400 were scattered around the city. In their mania to destroy everything Jewish, the Germans held nothing back in razing Jewish houses of worship to the ground.

The most magnificent was the Great Synagogue, which took from 1875 to 1878 to build. It stood outside the Warsaw Ghetto and was a true architectural masterpiece. On May 16, 1943, when the Nazis destroyed the Ghetto, they blew up the Great Synagogue. SS Commander Jürgen Stroop exclaimed with delight, "What a wonderful sight! I called out 'Heil Hitler!' and pressed the button. A terrific explosion brought flames right up to the clouds. The colors were unbelievable. An unforgettable allegory of the triumph over Jewry."

After the war, the only synagogue that remained standing

in Warsaw was the Nozyk Synagogue on Twarda Street. It was damaged in the 1939 German air assault but was not destroyed. During the war it was empty. Underneath the building was a large collection of books from all over Poland. Ironically, it was said the synagogue was useless because there were no more Jews in Warsaw. Yet under the building were stored more Jewish books than there were Jews in Poland. The Nazis eventually used the synagogue as a stable.

When the war ended, the building was restored and again used for worship. Halina was drawn there often to be among Jewish people and show her love and solidarity with the survivors.

As I stood at the back and looked over all of the heads, I prayed for them, asking the Lord of the Jews to bless them and to reveal Himself to them. One day, as I came in and stood with my Bible under my arm, I saw one of the men coming toward me. I recognized him as always being in the service, wearing his prayer shawl and kippah [skullcap]. As he approached me, I wondered what he would say when he learned that I was not Jewish. Perhaps he will tell me to leave. He might be afraid because he may think I am an informer from the police, sent to spy on them. And after all the Jewish people had been through, I could understand their concern. When he came close to me, he asked me a question.

"You are not a Jewess, are you?"

How I wished I could say, "Oh, you are mistaken. I am a Jewess." But this would not be true. So I answered, "No, I am not."

"Then may I ask what you are doing here?"

I liked his question, and I was prepared to answer it. I smiled at him and said, "I come here out of love."

"What? Out of love? Do you mean to say that you love Jewish people? My wife doesn't even like me because I am a Jew."

"I respect Jewish people. Moreover, I am greatly in debt to the Jewish people."

"You owe us a debt? Maybe I can help you then."

"That's very kind of you," I told him. "But you cannot help me. My debt is so great that nobody can help me. There is not enough time in an eternity to pay the great debt I owe the Jewish people. I showed him my Bible and said, "This Book is a translation of the Jewish Scriptures you have on the scrolls you hear read. They have led me to understand how to approach God. From this Book I learned about the only true God—the God of Israel. I also learned about the Messiah from the prophet Isaiah and other prophets. I learned how the Messiah, out of love, has given His life to pay the ransom for the sins of people. And even, I dare say, was crucified for my sins. And because I have accepted His sacrifice, I know that God has forgiven me. Because of this, I have not only Yom Kippur but eternal Kippur— eternal covering."

Then, after an extensive conversation, he asked me a question. "Tell me, please, are you the only person in Poland who thinks like this?"

"Oh, no," I replied. "There are many who think as I do—many." And then he asked me something that was like the Holy Spirit piercing my heart.

> *"If what you say is true, that you are so many, why do we never see such people here?"*
>
> *I left his question unanswered. But I was deeply moved to understand the great lesson I was being taught by the Holy Spirit. If you truly love someone, you will try to be with that person. So if we love the Jewish people, we will try to be with them.*

What Halina learned that day became the abiding principle of her life among the Jewish people. Friendship is better demonstrated by actions, rather than by talk, particularly with people who have experienced so much hatred, mistrust, and fear. Friendship must never be feigned to exploit someone. Nor should it ever be forced or used as a tool to gain an advantage. Trust is earned with time, patience, and sensitivity.

True Christianity is not something to be peddled or sold as merchandise. The Bible teaches, "For God so loved the world, that he gave his only begotten Son, that whosoever believeth in Him should not perish, but have everlasting life" (Jn. 3:16). True Christianity involves receiving a gift far too precious to be squandered, because it was offered from the deepest love known in time and eternity.

Halina felt privileged to demonstrate to Jewish people God's great love for them and prayed that someday they would understand it for themselves.

The words of the man in the synagogue haunted Halina for days. "If what you say is true, that you are so many, why do we never see such people here?"

The man was right, she thought. It was not enough to tell Jewish people they have Christian friends who love and pray for them; they need to be shown. She began asking herself how she could demonstrate that what she said was more than merely talk. She decided to be bold and go to the leaders of the synagogue and ask them what she and her Christian friends could do to help them.

"Rosh Hashanah, Yom Kippur, and Sukkot will soon be here. Could we perhaps help at the tables when you observe the feasts?" she asked.

"No, that will not be necessary. We can manage," the rabbi replied. "But I'll tell you what you can do, if you wish. The synagogue is in bad need of a thorough cleaning. In our synagogue are only old men and women who are barely able to get here for the services. If you could help us prepare the building, that would be much appreciated."

It so happened that when Halina was meeting with the rabbi and synagogue leadership, about 30 Christians were meeting in her home for Bible study. So when she got home, she asked them if they would like to help with the cleaning. Their enthusiasm was overwhelming.

After they had gathered cleaning supplies, brooms, and brushes and made soup for a hearty lunch, they marched like a small army toward the synagogue. People in the neighborhood must have wondered what was going on. They were accustomed to seeing squads of men with guns, but these people carried brooms and mops!

People at the synagogue were equally surprised. They were delighted to see so many Gentiles when only days before they wondered if there were any who were different from the Nazis and Communists. The three-day event was like a festival. Halina's crew scrubbed, polished, dusted, cleaned windows, and had the place looking like new before they left.

Cleaning the house of worship accomplished much more than anyone had anticipated. It broke the ice between the people of the synagogue and Halina and her friends. When Passover came in the spring, they were invited to join the Jewish people for the seder meal. In all, about 70 people attended and thoroughly enjoyed themselves. The Christian guests carried the food to the tables and heard appreciative comments. "When you come, the food tastes better," said one smiling diner. To add to the celebration, Halina and her little group had prepared a surprise. They sang a number of Hebrew songs they had learned especially for the occasion.

After returning to her flat later that evening, Halina reflected on how very good it was that, after so many years of regarding Christians as enemies, these wonderful Jewish people had met Christians who, in heart, mind, and ministry, were their friends.

Through Halina, God was doing a work in Poland; of that there was no doubt. But Communism was doing its work as well. The smattering of Jewish people left in Poland after the Nazi scourge had a very low level of comfort. It was not lost on them that Russia had been a hotbed of deadly pogroms and that Stalin's plan to unleash his own Holocaust to rid the Soviet Union of Jews was only stymied by his death in 1953.

Jewish people were scorned by the Communist authorities, who frowned on any celebration of the Sabbath or festivities associated with the Jewish holidays. Pushing their atheist agenda, the Communists wanted everyone to act like atheists whether they were or not.

Consequently, Jewish people were reticent to observe Shabbat openly or gather for the feast days. Halina and her friends knew that many Jewish survivors were still living under cover, fearing a return to the Jew-hating violence that had plagued them for so long. As she and her friends talked about the situation, Halina decided to open her home for a Passover seder. One of the young men suggested he ask his

Jewish friend, who was a student at the university, to come and lead it.

His friend was happy to accept the invitation. When the day came, he read the Passover *Haggadah* (the book that tells the story of the Exodus and contains the prayers and order of service) and led his hosts through a beautiful Passover service like the one practiced in his home over the years.

The next day, the student met with Halina. During their conversation he asked a question that had bothered him all night. "At the university, I very often meet Christians who want me to be converted from Judaism to belief in Jesus. But you did not speak about Jesus to me or make me feel that, to be your friend, I must be a Christian. May I ask why?" Halina answered him:

> *I told him, "If I had talked to you immediately about Jesus you would have rejected it because all of your life you have heard how Christians persecuted your people in His name. And many Jewish people still think of Jesus as the greatest anti-Semite, though in fact He was the greatest lover of the Jews and gave His life for them. I do believe that if you and other people will believe in God, the God of Israel, and turn to Him in prayer, He will reveal to you about Jesus of Nazareth—that He is the real Messiah for whom you wait."*
>
> *He said he was deeply impressed by what I had told him, and it gave him much to think about. As I thought about it, I was grateful that God has taught us not to make the Lord Jesus an issue until the Holy Spirit prepares the Jewish heart. Especially in places like Poland and other countries where they have been called "Christ-killers" and suffered so much by those identified as Christians. It takes patience*

> *and the work of the Holy Spirit. Pressure will only*
> *drive them away.*

Meetings at the flat for Shabbat services, Bible studies, and meals during the Jewish holidays went fine. But Halina faced a problem. Her ministry had grown so much that her flat was no longer large enough to accommodate all of the events and the group of dedicated believers serving alongside her. For years she had dreamed of buying a farm where she would have enough space for a fully functional ministry that could accommodate a lot of people and provide for their physical, as well as spiritual, needs.

One day, as she was reading from the book of Haggai, the Lord spoke to her through a verse of Scripture. It seemed to confirm her mission: "Go up to the mountain, and bring wood, and build the house; and I will take pleasure in it, and I will be glorified, saith the LORD" (1:8).

So the search began in earnest. At first, it seemed like a fruitless waste of time and energy. Halina was confronted by a series of letdowns—too small, too far from where it needed to be, or much too expensive. But despite the disappointments, Halina's faith never wavered. She knew God was in control. His schedule knows no interruptions or delays, and His timing is always perfect. She was confident He would lead her to a place where she could develop a full-scaled ministry.

Finally, in 1983, after countless hours of prayer and with the help of a host of friends in Poland and abroad who shared her dream, God led her to the perfect property. It was a 33-acre working farm with several buildings and plenty of room for more. After walking the grounds with several friends, Halina smiled and said softly, "I think we have found it."

Besides being big, the farm was in a choice location. It

was close to a highway and a short walk from a railroad stop where passengers, particularly Jewish people from Russia, could disembark. Halina suspected that big political changes were on the horizon. The Soviet Union was crumbling, and if God opened the doors to let Jewish people leave, they would leave in droves and need a place to stay en route to Israel and the West. She wanted them to have a comfortable place of refuge in Poland.

Even the words of the Jewish prophet Haggai took on an almost literal fulfillment as construction began. "Go up to the mountain, and bring wood, and build the house." A friend who actually lived in the mountains in the south of Poland had trees and offered to cut and deliver 80 of them for the house she later built on the grounds.

Between 1985 and 1987 construction took place on a structure big enough to lodge guests and someone to manage the farming aspects of the property. People were eager to help with the construction, and Halina experienced the wonderful feelings of joy and accomplishment so long suppressed by the Nazis and Communists.

Crude wooden benches were built so the volunteers could sit when they stopped to eat. At times more than 70 people showed up for work and enjoyed bowls brimming with hearty soup, along with so many loaves of bread that it taxed the ability of the kitchen staff to keep up with the hungry workers.

Everyone knew something more than mere construction was going on. They sensed they were participants in something big. God was doing a work, and they were a part of it. In the late 1980s, the iron doors of the Soviet Union unlocked, and more than 700,000 Jewish people were allowed to move to Israel.[1] In addition, more than 10,000 a month left the Soviet Union in early 1990.[2] At the farm, at least some of them had a place where they could rest for a while as they prepared to begin life again as free people.

The Soviet Union staggered to an end in 1991. By now Halina was 72 years old. She had experienced much in her life, but God was not finished using her yet. The Soviet Union's demise ushered in economic collapse and extreme hardship across the former Communist empire. Armenia, located at the foot of majestic Mount Ararat, had been a Soviet territory since 1921 and was hit especially hard. Jewish people in the capital city of Yerevan were suffering from a bitterly cold winter. They had no gas for heat and were starving due to a severe shortage of food.

Gustaw, who managed the farm, had contacts in Armenia. When he and a friend learned how the Jewish people there were suffering, they felt compelled to act. They quickly rented a plane, flew to Yerevan, and brought 150 people back to Warsaw where they were taken to the farm and housed until the Jewish Agency could arrange the group's passage to Israel.

The Armenians' stay at the farm was as joyous an interlude for Halina and her staff as it was for the immigrants. Halina's childhood desire to help Jewish people had finally become a reality. God was using the farm to feed them, help them, and care for them. And in doing so, He was fulfilling Halina's lifelong dream.

In a way, the farm represented a culmination for her. Yet it was only a beginning. Over the years Halina would arrange for busloads of Eastern European immigrants to use the farm as a temporary haven while they prepared to rebuild their lives in countries outside the former Soviet Union.

Meanwhile, she continued to receive invitations to teach about Israel in churches and speak of the Christian's responsibilities toward the Jewish people. When she spoke, she invited believers to the farm for the "Holidays With the Bible" conferences that had become an annual event. During the conferences, outstanding speakers were brought in to teach God's Word and explain His prophetic program for Israel and the world.

In time, she trained many young workers who fanned out in every direction to teach, sing, distribute literature, and bring to life the love of the Lord for a people too often treated with malice and contempt. Large contingents of Jewish and Gentile friends of Israel who had never seen the Holy Land began to go on tours guided by Halina's workers. And after walking the byways and ancient city streets of Israel, where the past fuses with the future, they came home with a contagious new spirit.

In a world that constantly speaks of change yet never seems to deliver, undeniable change has taken place—one life at a time—on a 33-acre plot dedicated wholly to the glory of God.

✍

For Halina, time was beginning to take its toll. On quiet evenings, she sometimes sat in her flat and remembered the carefree days when she and her friends chased miscreant boys on the playground. For years, life had been an adventure that promised so much. Then came the war and everything careened into chaos, darkness, and mass graves. Her Poland disappeared. Her family was shattered; and her life was stained by blood, fighting, incarceration, and suffering that could never be erased.

But Hitler and his henchmen were now dead. The Communist jungle of Karl Marx, Vladimir Lenin, and mass murderer Joseph Stalin was no more. And everything they had lived to destroy had survived. The State of Israel was a reality, and the Jewish people were back in their land. Poland was back and emerging as a vibrant nation. For all the Polish people had endured, they were at last free.

After all was said and done, the Bible Halina loved, based her life on, and trusted with all the strength of her being was corroborated by the history she had witnessed. A passage of Scripture stated the case perfectly:

Why do the heathen rage, and the people imagine a vain thing? The kings of the earth set themselves, and the rulers take counsel together, against the LORD, and against his anointed, saying, Let us break their bands asunder, and cast away their cords from us. He that sitteth in the heavens shall laugh: the LORD shall have them in derision. Then shall he speak unto them in his wrath, and vex them in his sore displeasure. Yet I have set my king on my holy hill of Zion (Ps. 2:1–6).

The King is coming, and He will reign exactly as He promised. That glorious truth was the abiding, stabilizing confidence Halina had lived by. Above all, there was the Messiah she loved and served—the One whose message of life and salvation she shared with so many who were estranged from their Maker.

Halina had answered God's call. She did what He had asked her to do. She ran the race that was set before her, always looking unto Jesus, the Author and Finisher of her faith (Heb. 12:1–2). Sometimes it had been difficult, and sometimes it had been lonely. But before she slipped off to sleep at night, Halina could say with perfect peace in her heart, "It was worth it."

[1] Steve Israel, "Broadening the picture—beyond America: Russia," The Jewish Agency for Israel <jewishagency.org/JewishAgency/English/Jewish+Education/Compelling+Content/Worldwide+Community/israeldiaspora/Russia.htm>.

[2] "Soviet Jewry Movement," Jewish Virtual Library <jewishvirtuallibrary.org/jsource/History/Human_Rights/sjmove.html>.

Epilogue

How does one craft a summation to a life so well lived? Perhaps I can accomplish that feat in some small measure by telling you about an incident that embodies the essence of Halina Ostik's story.

While I was executive director of The Friends of Israel, I traveled to Poland to visit the work. It was a pleasant day at one of the many children's camps Halina organized each year, and we were getting ready to take a group photograph of the Russian children who attended, along with their teachers. They had come to camp from Moscow and from a number of small villages, as well as from points beyond the Ural Mountains. For a week they had been learning the Bible and enjoying the many fun activities arranged by the camp directors.

This was the final day, and it was time for the children to make a presentation to the staff, teachers, and other visitors. The youngsters were beautifully dressed in costumes made at camp to represent their region and complement the performance they were giving that day. To the delight of everyone in the auditorium, Russian folk dances, Hebrew songs, little plays, and lessons from the Scriptures highlighted the program.

At the conclusion, the entire group was gathered for a picture. Seated in the center of the front row was Halina, ringed by dozens of smiling children with love in their eyes and joy on their faces. There it was: the perfect summary of an amazing life. Through all the ups and downs Halina had endured, even through the fire of World War II, her love for children never waned. The children represented life, the future, and everything that was right with the world.

169

Halina never forgot the pallid faces of the undernourished Jewish boys who had run past her mother and her on the street in Warsaw so many years ago. She had seen their faces again, or some very much like them, in the somber pictures that hung inside the entrance of Jerusalem's Yad Vashem memorial to the nearly 1.5 million Jewish children killed in the Holocaust.

Today the exuberant expressions on the clean and healthy faces of Jewish children who attend The Friends of Israel summer camps that Halina instituted are an image of hope and a promise of a better future.

In a way, the child held by the young mother in Nathan Rapoport's granite and bronze Monument to the Ghetto Heroes had made it through. If not actually, then certainly symbolically, in the final triumph that gave birth to a new generation of God's Chosen People. Halina's life contributed to that victory, and it was an investment that will return innumerable rewards.

Elwood McQuaid
June 2013

Other Books by Elwood McQuaid

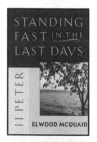

II PETER: STANDING FAST IN THE LAST DAYS

Time is running out. Our world is changing. Learn how to live for God in these last days, identify false teachers, and focus on eternity—all from the little but powerful book of 2 Peter.

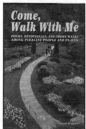

COME, WALK WITH ME
Poems, Devotionals, and Short Walks Among Pleasant People and Places

From the award-winning "One Nation Under God" to the celebrated "Death Meets the Master," this inspiring assortment of poems, minibiographies, delightful anecdotes, and devotionals will take you for a memorable stroll through time, countrysides, and the streets of Jerusalem.

FOR THE LOVE OF ZION

As Islamists relentlessly pursue jihad against all who reject the religion of the prophet Muhammad, many in the West are turning their backs on little Israel. But Israel will still endure. This book explains why, as it shines the light of God's eternal Word on the political and historical events of the Middle East.

IT IS NO DREAM
Bible Prophecy: Fact or Fanaticism?

Theodor Herzl, the father of Zionism, once said, "If you will it, it is no dream." Now you can scan the entire biblical prophetic program and see how a faithful, promise-keeping God molded historical events to make the modern State of Israel a "dream come true."

NOT TO THE STRONG

Journey to the time of the judges and examine four heroes of the faith whom God chose to turn the tide and deliver Israel. Their frailties may mirror your own—and what God did for them, He can do for you as well.

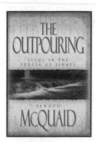

THE OUTPOURING
Jesus in the Feasts of Israel
God certified the credentials of the Jewish Messiah among Abraham's seed in connection with the great, festive commemorations of the Jewish nation. John's Gospel will come alive as you discover the magnificent relationship between the feasts of Israel and the Lord Jesus Christ.

PERSECUTED
Exposing the Growing Intolerance Toward Christianity
Staggering numbers of Christians are being killed each year. Why is there no outcry? Why no outrage? Elwood McQuaid shares eye-opening information and personal stories about people who are being persecuted for the sake of Jesus, challenging readers to break their silence. You'll discover how you can help those who risk everything for what truly will last forever.

THERE IS HOPE
Be encouraged by the wonderful events God has planned for His church. Learn why believers have no reason to fear the Antichrist and should look beyond the Lord's "coming with clouds."

THE ZION CONNECTION
Destroying the Myths—Forging an Alliance
This book takes a thoughtful, sensitive look at relations between Jewish people and evangelical Christians. It tackles such controversial issues as anti-Semitism, the rise of Islam, the right of Jewry to a homeland in the Middle East, and whether Christians should try to reach Jewish people with the gospel message— and how.

ZVI: THE MIRACULOUS STORY OF TRIUMPH OVER THE HOLOCAUST
This 2001 Gold Medallion Book Award Finalist is wonderful! It is the compelling, true story of how a 10-year-old Jewish boy survives the Holocaust, finds life-transforming faith in the Messiah, and becomes God's man on the streets of Jerusalem. It is a story you'll find difficult to lay down. Experience the history of modern Israel from 1948 to the present through the eyes of a miracle man in a miracle land.